WHERE DO YOU SPEND YOUR HEARTBEATS?

Design the Life You Desire,
One Heartbeat at a Time

STACEY AARON DOMANICO

Printed in the United States of America

First Printing, 2022

Print ISBN: 978-1-66785-884-5
eBook ISBN: 978-1-66785-885-2

Edited by: Kirkus Editorial
Proofread by: Linsey Doering

Published in the United States by: BookBaby Publishing

This is a work of nonfiction. While the events and anecdotes shared in this book
are real, the names of certain individuals and the identifying circumstances
associated with them have been changed out of respect for privacy. Therefore,
any resemblance to other individuals living or dead is purely coincidental.
Additionally, the content provided, while being offered in the spirit of
encouragement and general well-being, is not intended as a substitute for
the advice of medical or career professionals, or even your own intuition.

For my mom, who taught me strength.

For my daughter Sabrina,
who inspires me every single day.

And for all the women out there who are
overcoming obstacles, you've got this!

TABLE OF CONTENTS

HELLO!

Let's play the "What If You Only Had a Year Left to Live" game.
This is nothing new, of course. No doubt, this scenario has been posed to you before by some wise elder at a family Thanksgiving dinner or longtime friend over Saturday morning coffee at your neighborhood café. Your own romantic musings may even have prompted you to imagine yourself traveling the world, parachuting out of a plane, or tracking down the one that got away when you were in your twenties and about to build your life.

But I'd like to suggest that you take the Hollywood filter out of the picture. Now, zoom in and take a closer look.

At an average pulse rate of 80 beats per minute, this would mean having a little over 42 million heartbeats left in you. With each one, you are still alive. You are free to think, to make choices, and to create the life of your dreams. The shock of your imminent end aside, look inside your heart and ask yourself some tough questions:

- Where do you want to be?

- What dreams do you want to pursue?

- What do you want to do with your talents?

- With whom do you wish to spend your precious time?

- What words do you accept in your life, and which do you reject?

- Which issues do you deem petty and which worthy of your energy?

- Above all, how do you choose to treat yourself?

In other words, where do you spend your heartbeats?

With a turn of the lens, I bet you would suddenly see yourself and your life differently. You would know instinctively what your priorities were. You would see without question what was best for you. And you would immediately understand what you were all about. All those doubts you once held, all the fears you kept stored as if waiting for a famine—they would instantly vanish.

- Can you picture it—the life you've always wanted to create?

- Are you enjoying the kinds of friendships that add to your quality of life?

- Are you with that special life partner you thought existed only in your quietest of thoughts; the one you longed for so badly that you didn't dare hope for them?

- Do you feel joy surging through your body because you have that career or lifestyle you've always craved?

- What about the deep, calm breaths you're taking into your lungs each time you inhale? Can you feel them melting away the phantom walls of fear and anxiety you've spent years building like a fortress?

Now let me ask you this:

Are you really going to wait for a traumatic experience or life-threatening illness to arrive at your doorstep before finally taking control of your life?

If your answer is yes, you'd have a lot of company. It's what most people do. It's what I did. In fact, I waited until I had struggled through a soul-crushing first marriage and faced not one but two health crises before really sitting myself down and asking the hardest question I've ever been asked—by anyone:

Stacey, what are you doing with your life?

When I was forty-four, I was diagnosed with advanced breast cancer. But this was not my first shot across the bow from the universe. Just two years before that, I had been diagnosed with stage-zero breast cancer when doctors discovered calcifications scattered like holiday lighting throughout my breast ducts.

As if that weren't enough of a warning that my life needed to change, at that time I was in a marriage that was unhealthy at best, even though it was based on a foundation of first love and familiarity. Then one day, like a Formula 1 car heading for its next hairpin turn, I slammed on the brakes, and looked in the proverbial mirror.

Life is not supposed to be this hard.

It doesn't have to be this difficult.

It doesn't have to be this way.

From that moment on, midcancer and in midlife, I turned the wheel and found a different track, one that was made for me. And so began my healing.

Since then, it has been my dharma—my need—to help other people believe in who they are and the power they possess, long before a brush with death or some other life-shattering event takes place. If you are willing to take action, then I am here to offer you all the lessons I've learned, and all the strategies I've taken to get to where I am today; on my way to living the life I desire.

Before we continue, full disclosure: I am not a guru by any stretch. I am just another human being trying to figure out this earthly experience, and one who is still very much a work in progress.

While I have regained my health and am feeling stronger than ever, every so often I catch myself glancing over my shoulder when I'm about to have my next checkup. And there are other instances that remind me of the work I still need to do.

For example, I have the privilege of calling a beautiful house the home I now share with my forever husband, Ed. Walk through the front door on any given day, and you'll think it's just been professionally staged for a showing. We're talking fresh-cut flowers and all. But open any one of the junk-stuffed drawers, and something might just bite you. These are my "crunchy" parts, as Ed likes to call them.

Then there are past weight issues that began in my childhood. Today you'll look at me and see someone's who's got it together. Yet I still struggle with moderation and, yeah, occasionally I'll drink a little too much wine.

You'll hear all about this and more as I work with you and share my experiences. And while I may never get to that "perfect" place, I can tell you without blinking that I am so much closer now than I've ever been, and for that I am forever grateful for all that has come my way.

This includes, no big surprise, challenges in my childhood that chiseled at me almost daily. The spoiler alert is that this caterpillar eventually began its transformation to become a butterfly. While I am still growing the wings that will take me through this new phase of my life, I can't wait to share with you what I have already learned. These and other lessons I now offer you with a full heart, imperfections and all. However, even though I will be using my personal story as the foundation for this book, my ultimate focus is you.

We are here to help each other on our individual journeys. This I believe with every fiber of my being. Somehow, for some reason, my story has found its way into your hands, and I am honored that you've chosen to spend your precious heartbeats here with me. I don't have to remind you that there are no coincidences.

As you go through this book and learn about some of the hurdles I've crawled my way over (there was no smooth sailing for this girl, I assure you), picture yourself in your own human story and look for the parallels. I don't know anything about you, of course, but I can assume that you are someone with an open mind and a courageous heart. And that's all you really need.

But first, let's acknowledge a harsh truth:

It is far easier to hide from ourselves by being constantly busy instead of taking the time now and then to just *be*. We could live our entire lives this way without seeing or revealing what's really going on inside us. No one would have to be inconvenienced—including ourselves.

This is the path many of us—if not most—take. We ignore the obvious. We convince ourselves that the red flags are invisible, even though they're flapping so loudly you can hear them before you see them. We tell ourselves that our gut instincts are wrong. Have you ever done this?

- Have you ever taken stock of your life and looked back at all the messages you ignored?

- Have you ever wondered what your life would be like now had you paid attention to what your heart was telling you back then?

Look around you.

You witness this all the time: people sleepwalking through their lives, ignoring their dreams, doing their best to live small, even to remain invisible. They're trying not to see where and how they could turn things around. And for years, I did that too.

But no longer.

Today, I wake up each day, ready to make the most of my heartbeats. In those first few seconds, I see in my mind that I have just been handed a fresh juice box—the kind you'd toss in your school lunch bag or grab at the cafeteria. Then I see myself opening the juice box and drinking until the last drop is gone. By the time I'm finished, that box is so flattened, you'd swear a car had run over it. I now do my best to live like this every day, and I cannot imagine having it any other way.

I want this for you, too.

So, who are you? What brings you here?

Perhaps you're going through something serious—maybe even catastrophic. If that's the case, I know exactly how you're feeling. As someone who's faced near-stage-four breast cancer, I can tell you with sincerity that I have been in your shoes. But not only did I survive, I was blessed to find a path to healing that allowed me to live and move past the emotional trauma. It is because of this that I feel compelled to plead with you to never give up, no matter what.

But maybe your situation is not even that dire. Maybe you're "doing OK," and would be quite happy with that were it not for the voice inside telling you that you're not exactly clicking your heels each morning as you roll out of bed. If you're the kind of person who has the self-awareness to admit at least this much, then settle into a chair with a hot beverage, grab a throw, and get comfortable.

You're the person I want to speak to.

It is my hope to be the human speed bump that slows you down before you career headlong into a lackluster life—or, even better, the stop sign that brings you to a reflective halt.

Just as you don't need to have an accident before planning ways to prevent it, you don't need to wait until life has brought you to your knees before making a change. You don't need to hit that rock-bottom moment.

You can learn from others. You can learn from me here in these pages. Even better, you can learn from yourself.

With some raw honesty, hard work, and persistent focus, you can secure the pieces of your life long before they ever have to fall apart. You can become the kind of person who spends each heartbeat building a life that's everything they ever wanted it to be. You absolutely can.

"But how do I get there?" you might ask.

Let's turn the pages and find out.

1

WE ARE HERE
TO LEARN

Self-awareness. For some, the thought of looking within conjures feelings of enjoying a spa day for the soul. For others, dental surgery under local anesthesia. Either way, this kind of workout is similar to the kind you do at the gym. If you're fully engaged—i.e. not just posing in the weights section in an eye-catching ensemble by the dumbbell rack—you *will* strain and sweat. It can become uncomfortable because you will likely discover a side of yourself that you would rather not acknowledge.

It's not that we expect to be perfect, of course—no one is—but who readily admits to having traits (dare we say *issues?*) that are preventing us from having a life that's full? (Let's pause for the brave few to raise their hands.) That would mean taking responsibility for some of the questionable traits we have or decisions we've made. You know the ones—those that have our family and friends still shaking their heads?

Before we go any further, let me congratulate you for arriving at this point of your journey.

It is no secret that we are usually quick to give advice rather than follow it, especially when it's our own. We all know it is far easier to hold up the mirror to someone else than to look into one ourselves.

You see this all the time. The lecturer goes silent the moment they're being lectured. The secret fear is that if we look in the mirror, we may not recognize the face staring back at us. Then we wonder how we got here to begin with. Believe me, I am all too familiar with this feeling.

Just like going to the gym, however, dodging the real work will only cause your frustration to build. You know what I'm talking about—that nagging feeling that you're just not where you could be, that you're not being true to yourself. You may not even know where that "right place" is. You just know this isn't it.

So, if introspection triggers a sense of shame or angst within you, remind yourself that there can be no shadow without light. This means that you are already, at the core, a precious gem waiting to be unearthed. All you need to do is strip away the outer layers that shield your inner light from expanding. One way to do this is to see challenges in your life—whether through people or situations—as teachers.

LESSONS ARE EVERYWHERE

We are vibrations having a human experience. I believe this like I believe we need air to breathe.

Think about it. From friends to family to work associates to significant others, we are always either learning from others or teaching them about the knots that need to be untied so our joy can flow freely. I believe this is the case for us all.

But let's picture ourselves in the position of "student."

If we are always open to learning, it means that instead of reacting in a potentially negative way, we are more likely to pause, process, and pivot to view a challenge as a custom-made gift delivered to us in a different, if not unconventional, wrapping.

And what do we do when given a gift? We show appreciation.

With this approach, we can face the challenging encounter or experience with an open heart. Since I view this as I would when meeting someone for the first time, I call it the *Meet and Greet*. There are three steps to this process:

MEET AND GREET

1. Tell yourself that you've just encountered something interesting, and that you're about to learn a valuable skill or lesson. Remind yourself that even though you may struggle through some unpleasant moments, you will emerge wiser than before.

2. Identify the lesson(s) being sent your way. This will require you to remain calm and clear-eyed so you can sift through what initially may appear as random debris.

3. Let the lesson(s) flow through you without your biases filtering them. The conversation you have with yourself might sound like this:

"OK, Stacey. This person is being openly insulting to you. Why? What's all this really about?"

Or:

"It seems as if I usually end up doing all the work in group projects. Why? What energy am I putting out there that makes others think this is acceptable?"

Or:

"This person has me feeling irritated. Why do I feel this way when they're not even inconveniencing me? What's the meaning behind it?"

This last example is an interesting one. Here, no one is deliberately pushing your buttons. In fact, the other person has no clue how they're acting or how they're affecting you. Yet you're the one feeling somewhat off.

I am sure you've heard it said before that when people irritate you, it indicates that you may share the same or similar issues within yourself, issues you need to work on. Let me be honest—I always thought that this was just a cliché. Unfortunately, it's true.

In my working life, for example, I would come across individuals who sometimes made me want to gnaw at my nails. Over time, however, as I learned how to open my eyes and observe my own behavior in the mirror, I was able to see myself for how I really was.

One person, for instance, had a tone about them, particularly when delivering an ask. It was just a bit too sharp, and sometimes just downright unpleasant. But after stopping to look within myself, I realized that I, too, carried an edge to my voice when I had tunnel vision.

In fact, I was worse. I would go straight into the topic without first observing the usual social pleasantries such as "Good morning" or "How are you today?" *Wow! That's terrible! Do I really do that?* Once I recognized this, there was no hiding it. Yes, I was that person.

It was a hard lesson to swallow, but I was the better for it. And there were even tougher ones.

For example, I used to feel uncomfortable when in the company of someone who seemed to need a lot of attention. That sense of neediness that generally feels unattractive. Then, after taking a hard look at myself, I realized that I was no different. Let me tell you—I was having a lot of humble pie.

The good news is once I was further along in my healing and stopped needing attention, that trait in others no longer affected me as it did before. Instead, I would look at such people with compassion and quietly acknowledge that they were at a different stage of their learning journey. When you think about it, this is true for all of us.

Has this ever happened to you?

Have you ever watched someone's thought process or behavior, only to recognize yourself in them? It's humbling, isn't it? Remind yourself that we are meant to grow. As much as possible, remain aware. Become the observer and ask yourself the ultimate question: What is the lesson here?

As much as we hate to admit it, free will sometimes causes us to make decisions that simply don't help us in the long run. It's the reason we end up taking those unfulfilling jobs or choosing friends and maybe even life partners who are not truly aligned with us. They might be right for others, just not right for us.

MINING OUR PAST FOR GOLD

Do you have a moment to take a walk down memory lane?

When you look back, which memories have stayed with you? More importantly, how do you see them today? Permanently traumatizing or foundationally strengthening? If you find yourself still grazing at the buffet table of past hurts—and you know how we can gorge on that unhealthy fare—I'm here to tell you that it's never too late to turn those uncomfortable experiences into teachers.

NEW KID ON THE BLOCK

To help get you started, I'll share a personal story.

Like you, I'm sure, a few of my cornerstone lessons came early in life—during what I call my caterpillar years. When I was still in middle school and living in the Bronx with my mom and my sister, Deb, I battled extreme insecurities that led me down the path of obesity.

I was a classic case: The more I watched the other kids jumping around and playing—things I couldn't do—the more I ate. The more I ate, the heavier I became. The heavier I became, the more I withdrew. The more I withdrew, the more I ate. You know the spiral. By age eleven, I was four-foot-eight and over 150 pounds.

My mom, realizing she needed my dad's help, sent me to live with him for a few months in Maine, where he had settled after their divorce. Unlike my more free-spirited mom, Dad was all about structure. He also just happened to be a therapist by profession and was into fitness and health. I needed his life guidance like a pretzel needs salt. By the time I got to Maine, I was so overweight that he and my stepmother couldn't find ready-to-wear children's clothes that fit me. That, of course, didn't help with my self-esteem. Eventually, we had to go to Sears, where plus sizes were sold.

I was now the new kid at school, itself an angst-filled situation that could unsettle even the most confident child. It didn't help that I had already begun to feel homesick for my mom and sister. We had been the three musketeers for so long. Then, in my first week, I was faced with an experience that had the potential to shut me down indefinitely.

One day after school, on the short walk home from where the school bus dropped us off, the kids that lived on my block decided to have some fun at my expense. Still shy, I walked ahead of them, even though I had become friends with one of the girls, Beth. Without turning around, I could tell that she and the others were not far behind me. From the sudden lowering of their voices and the hushed snickering, I could also tell that they were now talking about me, and not in a pleasant way. You know how it is when you get that feeling.

Suddenly, in my periphery, I saw a stone whizzing past on my left. And then another. Finally, one made contact with my back. I flinched but didn't dare to turn around. That's when one of the kids shouted, "Jump up and down so we can feel the earth shake, Stacey!" Yes. He said that.

With my heart now close to punching a hole through my chest, I told myself to keep walking. *Just get home! Just get home!* Once alone and in the safety of our kitchen, I fell to the floor and unleashed a wail so primal, I was trembling. Seconds later, I heard a female voice.

"Stacey?"

It was my stepmother.

I had not expected to find anyone home. Ellen, also a therapist (I mean, how lucky was I?), usually would have been at work. As the universe would have it, however, she happened to be home that day just when I needed someone to catch me in their arms. Through gasping sobs, I worked my way through half a box of tissues while piecing the words together to explain what had just happened. She listened quietly. Then, when I was finished, she said the last thing I expected to hear.

"I think you need to go talk to Beth," she said. "Tell her how what happened today made you feel."

For a few seconds I stared at my stepmother, my face saying, *Are you crazy, lady?*

But in what would end up being a pivotal moment in my childhood, my stepmother put her training to work and got me to agree to confront the situation right away.

"Yes. You need to do this for you. Picture yourself standing in front of her and telling her how sad and hurt you are because of what she and the others did. If you speak from the heart, it will flow without effort."

For the next ten minutes, we sat there rehearsing the words I would use until I could see myself saying them without crumbling. This was, in fact, one of my first lessons in the art of visualization, a tool I would come to rely on later in life. For now, however, I was just a little girl who wanted desperately to stop feeling so sad. When the lump in my throat finally began to shrink, I took a deep breath.

"I'm ready," I said. Wiping my face dry, my eyes still red, I walked out the door to Beth's house.

Minutes later, I was standing before a surprised Beth. I said the words I had rehearsed only minutes before, wanting them to escape my mouth before I lost my nerve, or, worse, fainted. Once they were out and I had faced the fear, relief flooded my body. I had done it and was still standing. Then came the reaction I had not anticipated. Immediately disarmed, Beth's face softened as she apologized.

"Stacey," she said, her eyes growing wide. "Gosh, I'm really sorry. We were just playing around. Honest. We weren't trying to be mean."

Whether it was the innocence of youth or the side of me that wanted to believe in the innate good of people, I decided that Beth was being sincere and allowed the sadness of the past hour to dissipate. For the next hour or two, we played together, just two little girls having a fun time with Barbie dolls.

Thanks to a painful moment, I had discovered a muscle within me I didn't know I had all along. And while it would still take me years to develop it fully, it was a start.

• • •

Think about something you always wished you had handled a little or a lot differently. I'm not necessarily talking about heart-wrenching regrets. We'll talk later about staying clear of those. Instead, I'm referring to simpler experiences that still haunt you sometimes:

- Maybe it's a hobby you once enjoyed but dropped because it went from being easy to being difficult. Sure, you never planned to become a concert pianist, but had you stuck it out and found the courage to take those exams, you might be good enough today to entertain friends at home from time to time.

- Perhaps there's a moment when you caved to pressure and did something not quite in keeping with your character. It didn't get you in trouble, but you wish you had stood up to your peers and said, "No."

- Was there a business venture that never got off the ground because you and your partner were not on the same page? You wonder if it could have been salvaged had you spoken up sooner and voiced your concerns.

Are you there? Are you picturing those moments?

Now, imagine yourself handling the situation the way you could have. Do you see the outcome you desire? Of course, you do. I'll bet you've even rewritten the entire script all the way to the result you really desired.

As difficult as it may feel, it is better to find the courage to face your fear in the moment rather than choke on it for weeks, months, or even years. Why let fear eat away at you when it may be only an illusion in your mind? What a waste of heartbeats that would be.

If the reality turns out to be as ominous as you thought, isn't it better to find out sooner than later? This tool—the art of confrontation—is one I would learn to reach for often—first in my career and, eventually, in my personal life, albeit not soon enough. Today, I am generally known for being appropriately direct. There is very little now that I sweep under the carpet. By tackling life this way, I feel more at peace in general.

These moments of personal growth are important to experience, accumulate, and build on. As uncomfortable as they may sometimes be, embrace them. Let them show you how truly courageous you really are. Going forward, whenever life places a similar challenge on your path, you will remember those earlier touchstone moments and how it felt to solve a situation. It's like getting back on that bicycle after a nasty fall. The lingering fear will be counterbalanced by the knowledge that you have been here before. And with that, confidence grows.

WE HAVE THE POWER

I believe that, as human beings, we are all naturally programmed to learn, grow, evolve, and transform ourselves. Lessons, of course, don't just come through the people in our lives.

Other times, lessons come through an event—often traumatic—that opens your eyes and pushes you to your next level of growth. Ready or not, here it comes! While in the middle of figuring out my lessons in the context of my marriage to my high school sweetheart, along came my grand event.

A diagnosis like advanced cancer has the ability to change you forever. I say *ability* because, believe it or not, some fail to heed the lesson even when facing mortality. I was guilty of that with my first cancer diagnosis. So, when it came back for round two, I finally paid attention. I spent a lot of time with myself—and listened.

Physically, mentally, and emotionally depleted, not knowing whether I was going to live or die, I began to view my life differently. For the first time, I held up that mirror and asked myself some tough questions:

- *Am I happy?*
- *Is this really the life I want?*
- *Would I want this to be my legacy?*
- *If these were my final years, is this how I would spend them?*

This moment of honesty was soul-wrenching. It was one thing to know that my life possibly could end. It was quite another to know that, with the exception of having my beautiful daughter, I had squandered much of it up to that point. I didn't know which was more devastating. Honestly, it was all I could do not to fall into despair.

That's when I knew that I had finally learned the lesson.

"No," I said out loud. "No, I'm not happy. And I haven't been for a long time. This is not the life I want for myself. I want to change it. I need to change it."

To acknowledge that I had not been true to myself was one of the most humbling moments I had ever faced.

I sat with that acknowledgment. I allowed it to sink in and permeate every cell in my body as it struggled, literally, to survive. Then I asked myself the question: *What are you going to do about it, Stacey? Where are you going to spend your precious heartbeats from now on?*

That's when it all changed for me. I started reading every book there was on strengthening the immune system, learned about food as medicine and particularly about the relationship between sugar and cancer, and became interested in teachings about the mind, body, and soul connection, as well as the power of visualization.

Slowly, I began to heed the lesson that what we believe is what we create—whether good or bad. From that point on, I went to my chemotherapy sessions picturing the medicine melting the cancer cells. "Melt, melt, melt away," I'd say in a hushed breath. When I shared this technique with my new chemo friends at the center, we would all look at each other and whisper, "Melt, melt, melt."

I was going to survive this lesson no matter what. And then I was going to live the life I truly wanted. This was my new assignment—my forever project. And I was deleting the word *failure*, not just from my vernacular, but from my mind.

• • •

See your life as one gigantic classroom. Accept the fact that our enroll-ment will last until the moment we take our last breath. It may not be easy to do but it's that simple. Until that day, we're going to be tested over and over again. All of us. Open your heart and mind to all that your life is teaching you. See the lessons. Accept them with humility. Stretch. Grow. Evolve into that amazing light you know in your heart you are meant to be.

CHAPTER 1: KEY REMINDERS

- The secret fear is that if we look in the mirror, we may not recognize the face staring back at us. Then we wonder how we got here to begin with.

- If introspection triggers a sense of shame or angst within you, remind yourself that there can be no shadow without light. This means that you are already, at the core, a precious gem waiting to be unearthed.

- If we are always open to learning, it means that instead of reacting in a potentially negative way, we are more likely to pause, process, and pivot to view the challenge as a custom-made gift delivered to us in a different, if not unconventional, wrapping.

- Moments of personal growth are important to experience, accumulate, and build on. As uncomfortable as they may sometimes be, embrace them. Let them show you how truly courageous you really are.

2

FROM OBSESSION
TO POSSESSION

What's on your mind? What are you thinking?

We all know that our words matter, and we'll talk more about that in Chapter 7. For now, however, let's dive into our thoughts, especially those of the negative kind. We need to be just as careful with them, if not more. Because our thoughts go unheard, they often go unchecked.

How often do we heed this simple suggestion, only to revert to our subconscious thoughts without noticing? It's a struggle, I know. Our conditioning is strong—a resistance band made to tug us back with a snap without us even knowing. But if we are to build those mental muscles in order to transform our way of thinking, we must be vigilant and stretch ourselves beyond our current mindset. Because if we're not careful, we could very well bring about what we obsess about.

I'll start with a small example.

My mom is an amazing and strong woman—Bronx tough. When she was twenty-seven, a homemaker, and the mother of two young daughters, her marriage to her husband—my father—came to an end. This happened at a time when divorce was still a word that stuck in the throats of many and when married women still largely worked in the home. Still in the early phase of her adulthood, my mother suddenly found herself alone with two young mouths to feed. As a temporary bridge to a different life, and having little financial reserves with which to provide for her children, she went on welfare for a couple of years while she adjusted her sails and made both short and long-term plans to join the workforce. In time, she would indeed reinvent herself and make a life of her own. She was—and still is—a woman with enough gumption to spare.

As real-world sharp as this courageous woman was, however, she had allowed some of her internal tapes to work against her. They used to tell her that others were out to take advantage of her; that other than her friends, people were not to be trusted. I was, and still am, the opposite. I am trusting. In fact, I may even trust too much. I'll be the one in the supermarket walking around with my handbag wide open, practically begging someone to take my wallet or cell phone. *No one's going to take it,* I'll think. And no one ever does. Meanwhile, my mom used to have her handbag pulled tightly around her body. The result? You guessed it. People constantly gave her cause to doubt them. Once she changed her mindset, however, she changed what she attracted into her life.

There is something to be said about the energy our thoughts and words bring to us. Whether you're aware of it or not, our subconscious absorbs the messages we're downloading. You could even say that it's listening to us. And so is the universe.

LOOKING THROUGH THE KALEIDOSCOPE

Here's another snapshot from my childhood photo album.

After eventually returning to a healthy weight with the help of my dad and stepmother, I left Maine and went back home to the Bronx where I resumed my life as a city kid.

When I turned fifteen and started the tenth grade, however, crime in our neighborhood began making the evening news on a regular basis. (In fact, unbeknownst to us at the time, David Berkowitz—the serial killer known as the Son of Sam—used to live in the same apartment building as we once did.) My mom decided that we needed to make a home in a more stable neighborhood and set her sights north on Rockland County. By this point, she had completed her degree and was working full-time as a teacher. Between her income and a little help from our grandmother, we were able to make it happen. But because we did so midway through the fall term, I had exactly two weeks in which to prepare for midterms on course material I had not taken.

I was not happy. While I had always performed fairly well on tests, I was the kind of student that needed ample preparation. How was I going to pull this off?

The day after we arrived in our new home, I found myself alone on my bedroom floor, my books and study sheets scattered all over my bare room. With the moving van still days away with our furniture, I had none of the distractions that decorating a brand-new bedroom might have brought. Sitting there, my hands already sweaty from the panic building in my stomach, the world seemed to go gray as I told myself that I had no chance of passing the midterms.

And yet I wanted to—so very much.

It was then that I knew I had a decision to make: bomb or perform spectacularly.

In what I still consider to be another pivotal moment in my youth, I remember pausing to go within myself before doing something I had not done before: I viewed those midterms through a mental kaleidoscope and kept turning it until the situation no longer looked as bleak. In that moment, I locked into that feeling of doing well and let it expand in my heart.

As if with the flick of a switch, I was instantly infused with a sense of resolve and energy I had never felt before. A massive door had just swung open before me. Beyond its threshold was an expansive lightness and calm. That's when I knew it was going to be all right.

That's it. I'm gonna do it. I'm going to hunker down and pass those exams.

This ability to tweak my focus—my obsession—has become a go-to tool of mine. To this day, once I have decided on something, it has my full commitment—not just in words but in feelings. And when things get tough, as they often do, I remind myself that because I have done this before, I can do it again. That's when I return to the image of me conquering a past challenge—like becoming the boss of those midterms.

This life hack—being your own built-in cheerleader by acknowledging past accomplishments—is one way of using your thoughts to lift yourself up. It doesn't mean that you'll always succeed, of course, but knowing how to pat yourself on the back is a healthy habit. Because while there will always be people in your life to turn to for words of encouragement, what you really want is for your confidence to flow from you. You want it to be portable and on tap. But this essential quality often takes time to develop. You have to hone that muscle daily. And while experience is important, it doesn't always have to come from you. If you're observant enough, you can also learn from the experiences of others.

WARNING: *WHAT-IFS* STRAIGHT AHEAD

Let's enter the deeper realm of negative what-iffing.

We all indulge in this to some degree, don't we? Fortunately, 90 percent of what-ifs don't happen. That's the good news, and we'll take it. But what about those precious heartbeats you spent focusing on them? This includes attempts to mask your what-ifs with humor. You'll never get those heartbeats back. Wouldn't you have been better off channeling that time and energy on something supremely amazing?

If you're on the fence about the power of our thoughts, here are two stories you might remember the next time you catch yourself obsessing about something negative. While I can't offer you scientific proof of the cause-and-effect connection, I share them with you in the hope that it will make you stop and consider the possibilities. (Such as, *What if Stacey is right?*)

OK—YOU ASKED FOR IT

For most of my life, fear had been my constant companion. I can't begin to count the number of hours I would spend going down the rabbit hole of negative what-ifs. What's worse, my go-to obsession was, of all things, cancer.

Now, you're probably thinking that it runs in my family, hence the concern. No. While my mother did have a brush with sun-related melanoma, there is no history of cancer per se in our crew. I don't even know what planted this seed of self-destruction, only that it had taken root in my early adulthood. So strong was it in me that I would play something I called the "If This Happens Then I Will (or Won't) Get Cancer" game. I know. Crazy, right? Here are some examples of my inner conversations:

I'm in my car. As I'm about to approach a traffic light, I say to myself, *If the light stays green, I won't get cancer.*

Or:

I'm listening to a song and think, *If this song ends before the time turns to the next minute, I won't get cancer.*

Believe it or not, these were my daily tapes.

I worked my cancer obsession into my life any way I could. When I finally became a mom at thirty-three, the only magic wand I had to calm my daughter was my hair. As long as she could run her fingers through my long tresses, she'd stop crying. So, what did I do? I drew a straight line from that beautiful mother-child moment to cancer. *I must never lose my hair, so I must never get cancer.*

When I think back to the number of years' worth of heartbeats with which I fed this obsession, I almost feel ill. But that's what I did. Then, when I turned forty-two, I got my first cancer diagnosis.

• • •

That June day, I came home from work and did what most people do. I went to my closet to change into some comfy clothes; in this case, some loose sweats. It was time to relax with some wine and a nice green salad. (Who am I kidding? More like a pint of Ben & Jerry's Coffee Toffee Bar Crunch.) But this time, while changing, I noticed a few damp spots in the right cup of my bra. *Strange. Was I sweating? Did I spill something?*

I went on with my evening. But when it happened a few times afterward, I decided to see my real doctor instead of Dr. Google.

The next day, I called the doctor's office. When I described what I had been experiencing, the nurse practitioner asked if I could come in to see the doctor that afternoon. *Today? Wow. Sometimes I have to wait weeks to get an appointment.*

"Yes! I can come in today," I said.

I rearranged all my meetings, got there at 2:00 p.m. on the button, and saw the doctor. Two days later, I was at a restaurant at a coworker's birthday luncheon. After placing our orders, I checked my phone and saw a message from the doctor's office. They were now asking me to take a mammogram and sonogram. Inside, I froze.

I had always been good about having my annual checkup, but I wasn't quite due for the next one just yet. What did this mean? With a manufactured smile on my face, I politely excused myself from the table, called to make the appointment, and returned to my friends. I said nothing to them about my phone call. Still wearing my smile, the panic pushed down far from view, I did my best to swallow my meal. A few days later, I was sitting before the radiologist. Because I had "only" four microcalcifications in my right breast, they wanted me to return in six months to retest for any changes. Had I shown five, they said, they would be sending me for a biopsy. But that was too close for comfort.

"No," I said, "I'd like to do that biopsy now, please."

Inside, my head was spinning. *Why this? Why now?* As timing would have it, steps I had been taking up to this point to further my career were now opening doors. I was now in the process of being offered a promotion at work.

As much as I loved my career from the get-go, I had, up until this point, always held back on the gas pedal for two specific reasons. The first was that I was the mother and primary caregiver of a young daughter. This had been a personal decision for me, although I knew of many dynamic young mothers who had successfully advanced their careers while simultaneously doing an amazing job of raising their children. The second reason had to do with my situation as a spouse in an unhealthy marriage. (More on this in Chapter 3.) Because my life at home was energetically consuming, I needed to do whatever it took to keep my child happy and in as stable a family environment as possible.

At this juncture of my life, not knowing what the future had in store but feeling ready to step forward in faith, I had decided to say *yes* to my career and began interviewing in earnest. I felt this was a good step to take. So, when I had gotten the job as Director of Digital Marketing, I had literally jumped up and down with excitement. I had wanted this for so long, and finally, it was here.

Then, only a few days later, I got the call from the doctor's office.

"Please come in," they said. "We need to review the biopsy results."

Feeling that this might not be good, I decided that I didn't want to go in alone. I needed to have someone there to hold my hand, and there was only one person I wanted with me. I picked up my phone and dialed.

When you're in a toxic relationship, you spend a lot of energy pretending in front of strangers that all is well. If you've ever been in this kind of situation, you know that the show is as much for you as it is for them. But this time, I knew I wouldn't have the energy to pull off a stage show. The person I wanted to hold my hand the day I got my results was my wingwoman—my mom.

• • •

The office in Manhattan was practically magazine beautiful—clean and pristine. I remembered looking around at all the other women and telling myself that I would be just fine, all while noticing that I was the youngest one there.

When the nurse called us in, she led us to my X-rays laid out against a wall in front of a bright light. "Please sit down," she said to us, gesturing to the chairs. That's when she began to explain that I had DCIS (ductal carcinoma in situ), or cancer of the milk duct. But there was good news: At stage zero, it wasn't considered to be life threatening. Once an MRI confirmed that it was contained, all I would need was a lumpectomy and radiation. Listening to all of this, I felt as if we were ordering a sandwich with a side order of fries.

By this time, it was August and I had already started my new job, which I loved—and I mean l-o-v-e-d. I was getting to know the team, learning a different part of the business, and in my glory, tiara and all.

Then, one day, I was with a customer-focus group in the city when the surgeon's office called. The MRI tests showed the DCIS was throughout my breast.

"Your breast is like a clock," she said. "You have DCIS from three o'clock to nine o' clock. You're going to need a mastectomy." (Drop the mic.)

I processed the news as if doing shots—down in one gulp. *I have cancer. Cancer.* Because I never wanted to do this again, I asked for a double mastectomy. But once I made that critical decision and the necessary arrangements, I did an immediate swan dive into denial.

Our minds are stronger than we know. The best part is we get to decide how we use this power: to help us or hurt us. Sadly, my coping mechanisms were real and robust, and most of the times not the healthiest.

So deep was my denial that I told no one at work about my diagnosis. I shared it only with those who needed to know in order for me to arrange the time off I needed. I even convinced myself that I was having cosmetic surgery. That's right. I told myself I was having a boob job.

My first surgery did not go without a hitch. Major internal bleeding required a second surgery only hours later to stop the hemorrhaging, after which I was sent home to heal. *Whoo-hoo! It's all good from here!*

Then, just when you think it's safe to go back into the water, *boom!* Another wave hits you. A week later, when the pathology reports showed that the margins were not clean, I was forced to go under the knife for the third time.

OK. I can do this. I take on projects all the time at work. Massive ones. This is just another project.

Really?

When the third surgery and subsequent tests confirmed that the margins were indeed clear, I was told that it was unlikely—rare at stage zero—that the cancer would ever return. I was sent home with a fantastic prognosis and a broad smile on my face. According to the statistics, I had a 95 percent cure rate. It couldn't get better than that.

I had not, however, learned the lesson I needed to learn.

The day I got home, I picked up my life from where I had left off before my surgeries. In other words, I made no changes. I continued the same way of eating, worrying about what others thought, living in an unhealthy relationship, and treating myself like a foe and not a friend.

Healing, as I would eventually find out, is hard when you're not being authentic—when you're living a facade. Of course, I was too caught up in pretending to be happily married to understand this. So, I returned willingly to my fantasy world—to "normal."

Normal. An interesting word when you look at it. Two syllables. So benign-sounding. I would soon learn that there was no such thing.

I was still accepting less than I deserved and still being hard on myself. So much so, in fact, that when participating in a subsequent cancer survivors' walk the following year, I felt like an imposter. Yes, you heard me—I felt like a fraud. I told myself I didn't deserve to wear the survivor T-shirt, button and sash issued to each participant because I hadn't gone through chemotherapy. The other women wore hats or scarves. You could look at them and tell they'd had cancer. But not me. I still had a full head of hair. So, what did I do? I told myself that I didn't deserve to be called a survivor.

Well, the universe heard that too. *Oh, really? All right, then. You want to feel worthy? Let's see what it takes to make you feel like you really belong.*

Please understand—I'm not saying that this is what happened. What I am saying, however, is this: You must be the bouncer that stands guard at the gate of your beautiful mind. Scrutinize your thoughts before deciding whether to let them in. Be aware of the spirit of the messages you're sending yourself. Because, all day long, even while we're sleeping, our thoughts are constantly at work doing our bidding. You could say that our thoughts are our most faithful servants.

ABOUT DAD

Here's another close-to-home story that demonstrates the power of our thoughts.

My dad was the strongest, most vibrant, healthy, relentless, and structured man you could ever meet. The kind of person who lived his life out loud, he had but one fear: to end up—somewhere, somehow—in a nursing home.

He would often—and I mean, often—share this with my sister and me. We just couldn't understand it. *Why does Dad think that this would ever happen to him? He's so strong!* It was the furthest outcome from our minds. Sure, maybe it could happen to someone with an inactive lifestyle. But Dad? Impossible. He had always been ahead of his time, a fan of fitness and clean eating long before it became a popular lifestyle choice. Whether it was walking for hours along the beach or working out on the treadmill, he was always moving, and often competing with me for fun as I grew into an adult. In fact, exercising had become our special father-daughter bonding activity. To me—and to anyone who knew him—he was invincible. But for whatever reason, the fear of being immobile was real to him. Not only did it become his point of focus, it became his obsession.

Then, when he was sixty-two, he started to have trouble walking and remembering things. He assumed, of course, that it was just the normal aging process, until one day he could not remember how to tell time. That day was the beginning of the end.

After years of trying to find out what was wrong, he was finally diagnosed with Parkinson's with Lewy body dementia. As his life force was always strong, he kept pushing himself until he no longer could. He and our stepmother eventually moved into a smaller home with fewer steps and had a caregiver come in to help. Eventually, one caregiver became two, then two became around-the-clock care.

We wept as we watched him weaken and deteriorate to the point where he needed more care than we could give. It shook us to the core when we realized that the only solution available to us was a nursing home.

How? Why? What kind of cruel joke was this?

It did not seem possible, but it had happened. His worst fear—his lifelong obsession—had come true. Then, when we thought 2020 couldn't get worse, it did. My father passed away from COVID-19 in December of that year, one day shy of his seventy-eighth birthday.

CHERYL'S STORY

Think about those you know with similar stories.

A friend of mine, Cheryl, recently shared that, for as long as she could remember, her mother had worried openly about losing her sight in her old age. "I'm so afraid of going blind," her mother would say over and over again. At first, Cheryl paid no attention, assuming that this must have happened to a relative in the family, one she had not met back in Europe, where her mother was from. But one day, as her mother's sixtieth birthday approached, Cheryl finally brought it up.

"Mom," she said, "does blindness or some other serious eye disease run in the family? Is there something we need to look out for?"

Much to Cheryl's surprise, her mother replied, "No, not that I know of. I've just always been afraid of going blind."

Cheryl was not just puzzled, she was upset. Why focus on something when there's no evidence to support the likelihood of it happening? What a complete waste of energy! But when her mother developed macular degeneration in her late sixties, Cheryl all but went into shock.

"The hairs on the back of my neck stood on end," she said.

REWINDING AND RECALIBRATING

What is your worst fear? How much time do you spend thinking about it? Be honest with yourself. And do you really want to continue feeding it with your energy? No. You have the power to stop it in its tracks. You can choose to spend your heartbeats in ways that better serve you.

If you have a particular fear that quietly stalks you, you're not alone. We may joke about it, but many of us have something we secretly dread. For example, how many of us know someone who pictures plummeting to their untimely end as soon as they get on an airplane? You get the idea. It's normal to have fears. The trick is not to let them take control of you. There's a way to turn this around.

Now, when I find myself even mildly entertaining a negative image or scenario, I immediately rewind that image and recalibrate my energy around it.

Let's try this together. I'll give you an example so we can walk through it.

Here's the fear:

"I'm afraid of becoming a recluse in my senior years like the neighbor down the street. She lives alone, seems to have no family or friends, and goes nowhere."

1. Lean into your fear as if watching a movie. See yourself alone in your house day after day. Feel the isolation. Feel the loneliness.

2. Hit "Pause" on this thought and freeze this image. Take a good look. Tell yourself that it doesn't have to be this way. Tell yourself that this will not be your life's standard.

3. Now, what's the opposite of this fear? Picture it in your mind.

4. Zoom in and see what that would be like. In this new scenario, you're constantly surrounded by family and friends. Everyone wants your attention. You're always going out to social events and must sometimes decline invitations. The phone rings often. *This* is the picture you want.

5. Hit "Rewind" and keep replaying the new thoughts until you are fully immersed in this new scenario you have just imagined. Don't stop until you get there. This is what you long for. It is the opposite of your fear in every possible way.

6. Recalibrate your thoughts and energy around this new image. From this moment on, this is your standard and your story. Whether through affirmations, self-talk, or visualization, you will diffuse all thoughts of that old fear until it no longer exists. No reruns will be allowed. From now on, you have a new story.

• • •

We have the power to create our life experiences, whatever you want them to be. Look around. There are beautiful examples of this everywhere. As for me, today my mantra—my focus—is different. I tell myself that I am healthy and loving the life that I have designed. And so, I ask again. What about you? What are you thinking? What's really on your mind?

CHAPTER 2: KEY REMINDERS

- Our conditioning is strong–a resistance band made to tug us back with a snap without us even knowing. But if we are to build those mental muscles in order to transform our way of thinking, we must be vigilant and stretch ourselves beyond our current mindset. Because if we're not careful, we could very well bring about what we obsess about.

- Whether you're aware of it or not, our subconscious absorbs the messages we're downloading. You could even say that it's listening to us. And so is the universe.

- There will always be people to turn to for words of encouragement. What you really want, however, is for your confidence to flow from within you. You want it to be portable and on tap. Our minds are stronger than we know. The best part is we get to decide how we use this power: to help us or hurt us.

- Be the bouncer that stands guard at the gate of your beautiful mind. Scrutinize your thoughts before deciding whether to let them in. Because, all day long–even while we're sleeping–our thoughts are constantly at work doing our bidding. You could say that our thoughts are our most faithful servants.

3

HANDING OUT THE RIGHT INSTRUCTION MANUAL

You've heard about kids going to their friend's or grandma's house and behaving like angels, only to return home and transform into miniature monsters the moment they step through the front door. If you're a parent, you've probably had this happen to you. How do even little kids know instinctively how to adjust their behavior accordingly? We teach people how to treat us. This is not news. The question is, do we really take note of the instructions we set for others to follow? If we have examined this aspect of our lives only to discover that we have been sending the wrong signals, do we ever do anything to correct them?

As difficult as it is to accept, the truth is that for every relationship we have—be it with family, friends, coworkers, neighbors, and especially our significant others—we set the rules of engagement. We are at the controls.

To make this universal truth stick, let's phrase it another way:

People will treat us the way we ask them to.

How well have you done in this area of your life? Think about the following questions and be as truthful as you can. Remember, the only person listening is you.

1. Without stopping to analyze it, how would you describe your boundary-setting skills as it stands at this moment? Rate it on a scale of 1 (low) to 10 (excellent).

2. Think about those individuals with whom you are close (e.g. relatives and friends) or are in constant contact (e.g.

colleagues). Jot down their names to make sure you have accounted for everyone.

3. How do you feel about yourself when you are with these individuals? How do you feel even after you've left their company? Do you feel heard, respected, appreciated, important, supported, uplifted, relaxed, energized, or limitless? Or do you feel dismissed, invisible, taken for granted, used, depleted, tired, confused, small, or anxious?

If most of your emotions fall in the first group, congratulations for establishing healthy boundaries. But if you find that the second group best describes your current feelings, don't despair. If you really want to turn things around, you can.

A TALE OF TWO SOULS

How?

That was the word that kept coming to me each morning I woke up in our new home in upscale Rockland County, after our mom had decided we needed a different life.

Like a figure on a Monopoly board, I felt as if I had been plucked overnight from our Bronx neighborhood and dropped right on Boardwalk. And while on the surface I was making the adjustment well enough at my new high school and neighborhood, I struggled with deep feelings of unworthiness.

Beneath the outward smiles and laughter, I was busy sending myself the usual assortment of unhealthy messages:

- *You don't deserve all of this.*
- *They're going to figure you out real soon.*
- *You know you don't really belong here, right, Stacey?*

That was me then, my ego constantly on overdrive looking for all the ways I had messed up in the past or would in the future. My self-image—and therefore my treatment of myself—was nothing short of shoddy. The problem, of course, was that it didn't end there. Our self-image—whatever it may be—is the user manual that informs people about how we see ourselves. Whether we realize it or not, we consult this manual every day with every interaction, word, look, and gesture to teach others how to treat us.

SETTING THE RULES OF ENGAGEMENT

Within six months of moving to our new home and settling into our new life, the unimaginable happened. I found myself a boyfriend—my very first. Smart, attractive, and a natural charmer, my high-school sweetheart all but scooped me up from the moment we met through a mutual friend at the New City condo benches.

Extremely attentive and engaging, Tom made me feel as if I had won a raffle—a prize I thought I had no chance of winning. It was a sensation I had never experienced before. I couldn't have known it, of course, but with all the abandonment issues I had brought to my new life along with my clothes and bedroom furniture, I was completely susceptible to his overtures. Were they even overtures, though?

The truth was he needed no real effort to pull me in. With our particular set of childhood issues and conditioning, we were two strangers who sensed an immediate familiarity in the other. We could have been blindfolded and led into a room filled with people and still found each other.

What was there to be suspicious of? My amazing boyfriend came from the kind of family that had a house with a pool, a Jacuzzi, and dinners that were eaten at the dinner table—a table set with a tablecloth, cutlery, pretty plates, glasses for water, and even glasses for wine like they did in restaurants.

From the start, I acted as I felt: as if I was the one who had lucked out. That, of course, was my first set of instructions to Tom: *Treat me as if I'm beneath you.* It should also have been my first red flag indicating that this relationship was based on a shaky foundation. But what did I know at fifteen about such things? What does anyone know at that age?

I look back sometimes and wonder if it could have gone any differently. If I knew of a magic potion that would make these inner messages appear over our heads like flashing hologram speech bubbles, I would set up shop immediately. Today, when I see young people starting out their journeys while ignoring their red flags, I want to grab them by the shoulders and shake them until they see what they're doing. But all is not lost. If you missed the warning, the next best thing to do is learn from it.

Convinced in my fifteen-year-old head that Tom was "the one," I accepted everything while questioning nothing. And then came the new assortment of daily recurring messages: *Boy, did you ever get lucky! He probably feels sorry for you. Don't mess up, or he'll leave you.* And, of course, there was the headliner: *This is your only chance—you won't ever find anyone else.*

Like a creature at the bottom of the sea dependent for survival on morsels from the top, I had fallen deeply for Tom and his world. His life and family were unlike anything I had known, and yet there I was, being welcomed with open arms to join them. I jumped right in.

Strangely, what had the biggest impact on me was the family dynamics at dinnertime. Growing up with a mom who had no choice but to work full days and then some, TV dinners—eaten in front of the TV, of course—were our main fare. I don't think Tom's family even knew what a TV dinner looked like. They gathered as a family to eat *and* talk. The first time I experienced this, I sat bewildered, looking left and right as the conversation bounced from person to person. *What's wrong with these people? Don't they know how many sitcoms we're missing right now?* But by the end of the evening, I was hooked on what felt like a cohesive family life.

Tom and I dated throughout high school and had a relationship heavily punctuated with mood swings and outbursts, all of which I condoned by staying in it. Over and over the cycle continued like a broken record. After a while, like adjusting to the ambient temperature, I gradually acclimated to what was clearly a toxic situation.

The years passed. Finally, it was time for me to go to college. But when I expressed interest in pledging to a sorority, my boyfriend issued me an ultimatum.

"Pledge and we're over," he said.

This time, in what was a rare moment of centeredness in my youth, I did the healthy thing and showed him my boundaries.

"Buh-bye, then!" I told him. And pledge I did to a group of women who continue to be like sisters to me to this day.

Eventually, however, those resistance bands snapped me back to Tom and my comfort zone. I would argue that a better term in this case would be *familiarity zone*. Living on eggshells is anything but comfortable. When I graduated, I returned home to find that he had moved on with another girl. That, of course, should have been another clear sign that I needed to move on once and for all. Instead, I looked the other way, returned to those shaky boundaries of mine, and agreed to let him see us both: me on Fridays; the other girl on Saturdays. (I hope you're cringing as you read this.)

At the time, I was rooming with three other girls in a house we rented. "Why are you even putting up with this?" they asked, the looks on their faces suggesting that I had arrived from another planet. But instead of walking away as I should have, I eventually told Tom he had to choose. It was her or me.

I thought I was being mature about the situation. Today, of course, I know better. By agreeing to stay in a relationship in which I was an option and not a priority, I was essentially telling this person that a part of me was willing to accept treatment I did not deserve.

Four years later, we got married.

Even as we walked down the aisle, and even though I genuinely cared for this man who had been my first love, I knew something was off—with him, with me, and with us. Instead of dealing with it, however, I sought distraction and buried myself in my work. It was the one area of my life to which I could escape and really flourish. But even that triggered his extreme mood swings and constant need to control. If I was soaring, he'd find a way to push me down. Catering to him—particularly when done in public so as to thwart any potentially embarrassing blowups—only seemed to egg him on.

Before long, like staring longingly at something you want in the display window of your favorite shop, I found myself observing other couples when we were out and envying them. I'd see how kind they were to each other. How they'd talk, laugh, be playful, and how they seemed to genuinely like each other's company. They reminded me a lot of my dad and stepmother. He and Ellen had that playfulness about them. Wasn't that how it should be? In my heart, I knew that my husband and I did not have this connection. It was something I so desperately wanted.

In the interest of those readers who aren't familiar with the dynamics of a toxic relationship, I want to digress a moment to say that identifying the core issue in a toxic relationship is not as simple as you might think. It is not always clear-cut. For as cruel as someone can be, they also can be equally kind. It is this pendulum swing that plays with your mind.

Not a birthday went by when Tom didn't treat me like a queen. Even during my chemo treatment, which came during round two of cancer, he showed what I still consider to be true kindness.

I was so sick that Thanksgiving that he rubbed my feet as I lay in bed, barely able to move. Yet this same person had the capacity to say things so hurtful, that I once found myself sliding down the wall to the floor in hacking sobs as he berated me the day before my double mastectomy. I share all this to say that those of us caught in this kind of relationship spend much of our waking hours questioning our sense of judgement, if not our own sanity.

But the entire time, more than anything, maybe even more than my battle for life, my focus was on my daughter. I felt her eyes on her father and me. I knew she was watching my every move, watching me teach her father how to treat me.

Like most individuals in a troubled marriage, I stayed at first for the sake of my child. Being from a broken home, I was determined to do "better." But I eventually realized that I had to leave—for the sake of my child. If she was to have a real chance at having a healthy relationship with a significant other in the future, I needed to show her how strong we can be, not just as women but as human beings. I needed to show her what self-respect looked like, and what real joy, fulfillment, and unconditional love felt like. Because we all deserve to find happiness.

Her father and I—through no fault of our own—did not bring out the best in each other. I did not want my legacy to be the image of a wilted soul willing to remain stuck. I didn't want my little girl wondering—potentially for the rest of her life—why Mommy let Daddy treat her like that. I didn't want her wondering why her mom didn't find the courage to fight for her own happiness.

It was at this point that I began to question everything while pushing the cancer back and out of my body. I took every class the hospital offered: yoga, meditation, and psychotherapy. For the first time, I took a serious look at food as medicine. In particular, I learned about the relationship between sugar and cancer.

Then, one day, after another exhausting chemotherapy session, I stopped to look at the image in the mirror. I saw someone who was weak, bald, and tired. So tired. Seconds later, the tears came pouring down. Staring into the soul of my being, I looked into my eyes, now bare and vulnerable without their protective eyelashes. In that moment, something switched. For the first time, I began to really understand what it meant to love myself. I began to talk to the frightened little girl who still lived within me.

I'm going to take care of you, I told her. *Everything's going to be all right. I'm here for you now.*

I was at a crossroads. My life had to change. Even if it took one decision at a time, one day at a time, one heartbeat at a time, I would make it happen.

My husband and I had said the word *divorce* many times for years, usually during a heated argument. I knew in my heart that once I was physically strong enough, I would leave the marriage. I was grateful for all the lessons we had learned together. There would always be a special place in my heart for Tom, but the time had come when I had to put my health first.

A few months later toward the end of March, I graduated from chemo, rang the bell, and enjoyed the little celebration they throw for you with—um—cake. (Cake? Oh, I'm not falling for that sugar trick!) My next step was to have a PET scan to determine whether the chemotherapy had done its job. If the scan showed that all was clear, a couple of months of radiation would follow for good measure. In preparation for the PET scan, I had to avoid carbs the day before because you're injected with a glucose-type liquid to see if anything lights up. (Glucose? Finding cancer? That just reinforced everything I was reading about the fact that cancer feeds on sugar.) Once that was behind me, I had the dreaded wait for the results. To this day, waiting for medical test results still has the power to make me feel as if Earth has stopped spinning.

And so it was that on a warm spring day, the doctor's office called as I was walking up the stairs to my bedroom. I stopped, dropped to the step below me, answered the phone, and closed my eyes.

"Congratulations," the nurse said. "The PET scan is clear."

Tears began streaming down my face. I wanted to shout my happiness into the stratosphere. Seconds later, I was openly sobbing with relief. I had been given a second chance. This time, I would not waste those heartbeats. I was going to reach for the life I deserved. Even as I went through radiation and the search for creams to help with the burning (yes, it's a thing and a hot topic with radiation patients in the waiting room), I smiled with a joy so powerful that I could almost feel it coursing through every cell in my body.

The months went by, and soon it was summer. Everywhere I looked, there was rebirth: the buds of the trees, the flowers, and me.

My radiation treatment now over, my hair began growing back. At first, it only started reappearing on the sides with nothing on top, which made me convinced that I was going to look like an eighty-year-old man for the rest of my life. But I didn't care. I had life. *Life.* And for that, I was grateful.

Slowly, my body began returning to health. Now back at work, I reveled in everything the world had to offer—even traffic. I learned how to have more patience, empathy, and gratitude. This time, I looked at things differently. Now I saw my life as a bank account filled with heartbeats. I started paying close attention to where, with whom, and how I spent them. The latter included how I let people treat me. I was ready. No longer was I the same person who had started this journey.

It was time to align.

One morning, I woke up, put my wig on, and drew in my eyebrows. (They took a long time to grow back, and the eyelashes even longer.) After putting on a simple outfit and checking my image in the mirror one final time, I picked up my purse and drove down to the lawyer's office.

TAKING INVENTORY

The assessment of my life extended beyond what would eventually become my former marriage. After setting the paperwork in motion, I turned my attention to those in my life—family, friends, and even work associates. Now comfortable with honesty, I had to admit that, yes, I had allowed people who were energy vampires to come into my life, and stay. It was almost always about them and how I could best fill their need for attention. This job had become, quite frankly, exhausting. While I had done this willingly in the past, I now wanted to live my life with more self-respect.

I began to pay close attention to who and what made me unhappy and deconstructed each situation by asking myself what was behind it. What was it that did not sit well with me?

One by one, I practiced putting limits on how deeply I would engage with these individuals, all of whom I cherished, but now needed to love on healthier terms. Meanwhile, I began spending time with people who were on my vibrational level.

And then it happened.

Like a tap that had been opened, this incredible flow started pouring through my life. Suddenly, it all became so simple, so easy. That was the moment I understood that this was how it was supposed to be. This flow—this ease of just *being*—was the way we were meant to live.

- If it's right, there is no pressure.
- If it's right, it feels like play, not work.
- If it's right, it's energizing, not exhausting.

What does this look like in real life?

It means having friends who don't give you a guilt trip for not texting or calling them back as quickly or as often as they'd like. It means having work colleagues who want you to succeed. It means having a significant other who encourages you to go for that promotion instead of instilling doubt about your ability to learn new skills or take on bigger challenges. Because if someone loves you unconditionally, they want to put their arms around you to help lift you up, not keep you down.

• • •

Today, I take care to ensure that even my words help to teach others how to treat me. For example, in the past, I used to hand out apologies as if they were candy:

- Have to give someone an answer you don't want to hear? *I'm so sorry!*

- Wasn't able to call when someone wanted because I had a previous obligation? *I'm so sorry!*

- Can't go shopping with a friend on a moment's notice? *I'm so sorry!*

I also used to catch myself offering an explanation even when none had been asked of me. It was an indirect way of assuming that I owed the other person an apology. Now, I reach for truthful but respectful phrases that do not include the reason(s) behind my decision:

- "A meetup this week doesn't work for me, actually. Next week would be better."

- "Thank you—I'd love to attend your party, but can't make it this time."

- "Yes, I can help you move to your new apartment this weekend, but only for a few hours on Saturday morning."

Then I allow the pause or silence to fill the air.

I want you to try this the next time you find yourself in a similar situation, when you're tempted to apologize for fear of upsetting someone else:

1. Mentally clamp down on your tongue so that the other person is forced to break the silence. This also helps to ensure that you do not make promises you can't—or don't want—to make. Until you become more comfortable with this, you will feel that old temptation to explain further. Resist the urge.

2. If you do have a knee-jerk reaction and automatically agree to the request being made, call the person back as soon as possible and be honest. You can say, "I've had a chance to look at what's on my plate at the moment, and I don't think I can agree to do that as I first thought."

3. At the end of the conversation, make a note of how you're feeling. If you spoke from the heart—from a place of truth—you should notice a lightness about you. In fact, you should feel the absence of that heaviness that settles in when you know you have (once again) agreed to something you simply don't want to do.

Let's be clear. If you are absolutely, positively, 100 percent sure that you can and want to make yourself available to someone, fantastic. But if you have even a tinge of hesitancy, buy yourself some time. If you know you're a recovering people pleaser, not only do you want to create a delay, you should take it a step further and use each opportunity to retrain your way of thinking. This way you teach people that you are considerate, not just of others but also of yourself.

How do you do this?

Prepare ready-to-use phrases and rehearse them in your mind. Use them as your default delay responses.

DEFAULT DELAY RESPONSES:

- "That sounds like a real possibility. I'll get back to you to confirm."

- "I'm almost sure I can, but I'll confirm with you as soon as possible."

- "I'd love to! First, let me check something before I commit."

Tone and word choice are important here. Notice how the above examples land on your ear—friendly but firm. They stick. There is no room for discussion. As much as we hate to admit it, however, decades of insidious conditioning still have many women using tone and language that suggest to others that they can be swayed. See if you recognize any of these examples.

LANGUAGE OF WEAKNESS:

- "I suppose."

- "I guess."

- "I think I might."

What happens when we speak like this? Oftentimes, we are railroaded. This is easily corrected by delivering your message in language that is firm but with a tone that's pleasant.

Don't say: "I think I might want to leave the dinner party by ten p.m. because I have an early morning the following day."

Do say: "I plan to leave the dinner party no later than ten p.m."

When you think about it, this show of authenticity honors both involved. For one, whenever we bring our truth to any interaction, the other person feels that we have faith in them. By being honest, we are telling them that they deserve only our best. When we use our heart-beats in this way, we build our self-respect. If you remember nothing else, remember this: It is your right to change your mind.

This is not to say that the other person won't take offense. Some will. But those are the same people who perceive a slight whenever their wishes are not met on their terms, no matter the situation. Once you stop bending to please these people—once you have shown them how you wish to be treated—they will stop coming around as often, or at all. Even better, they may even learn to respect you and adapt to the new dynamics of their relationship with you.

So, ask yourself the tough question: Are you happy with the way others treat you? Do you find that you're constantly being bullied in small ways, even by those who genuinely love you? And by "bullying," I mean boundaries being crossed, often in the name of "closeness" (e.g. "I know you won't mind, but I volunteered your help to a friend's charity," or "I hope you don't mind, but I lent your book to my neighbor for his upcoming trip to Cancún"). Understand that they don't overstep because they're "bad" people. Yes, they may have their issues to sort out, but they're merely following your signals. All along you've taught them what you will and will not tolerate.

• • •

You've lived your entire life teaching others how to perceive and treat you. Going forward, you can rewrite your instruction manual. Take small steps if a complete and sudden change scares you. If you do this from a place of love, the people who want to stay in your life will not only stick by you, they will respect you even more. In fact, I dare say they'll be mighty proud of you.

What's more, you'll be proud of yourself.

CHAPTER 3: KEY REMINDERS

- Our self-image–whatever it may be–is the user manual that informs people about how we see ourselves. Whether we realize it or not, we consult this manual every day with every interaction, word, look, and gesture to teach others how to treat us.

- Pay attention to red flags. Instead of ignoring those messages from our gut, picture them appearing over your head like hologram speech bubbles.

- See your life as a bank account filled with heartbeats. Pay close attention to where, with whom, and how you spend them.

- This flow–this ease of just *being*–is the way we are meant to live.

- Identifying the core issue in a toxic relationship is not as simple as you might think. It is not always clear-cut. For as cruel as someone can be, they can also be equally kind. It is this pendulum swing that plays with your mind.

4

♥

LISTENING TO
THOSE MESSAGES

I have a confession to make.

When I was still in the early stages of writing this book, I got a case of cold feet and hit the "Pause" button, even though I knew in my heart that I was meant to share my story to help others. Of course, knocking at my door were all the fearmongering what-ifs that had come for coffee and conversation.

Honestly, I was a little embarrassed. There I was, writing about facing our fears, telling my readers how to create and design their lives to be expansive, and showing them how powerful they are. And yet I was wiping the cold sweat off my own brow and questioning my plans. *Really, Stacey? Even after facing the big C?*

I spent a lot of time processing this. I did not react, did not draw up a pros-and-cons list, nothing. Instead, I turned to a process I had developed for myself—a tool—to help me when making important decisions. It's a simple five-step process I call my *Stethoscope Gut Check.*

- Is there a decision you need to make?

- Something you're wrestling with?

First, think of a decision that's currently on your plate. Perhaps it's work-related—a new position you're considering that may mean more travel, longer hours, or relocation. Maybe it's personal—a relationship that you either need to save or end. It could even be something as simple as whether or not to get that red sofa you've been thinking about or keep the tan-colored one you've had for years.

Are you ready?

STETHOSCOPE GUT CHECK

1. Imagine yourself going with one decision. Really see yourself going down that direction. Picture everything that comes with it: the people, the location, change of pace, the weather, the sounds, smells, maybe even a change of language or culture. *Feel* yourself being immersed in it. Then take a deep breath, and listen to what your gut is telling you. Notice your feelings for what they are. Don't judge or try to understand them.

2. Picture yourself going with the other decision, and dive into it as deeply as you did above. Take another deep breath, and listen to what your gut has to say about that scenario.

3. Take note of which option makes your body feel instantly calmer. Observe your breathing again. Which situation feels more freeing? Which causes your shoulders to relax? Which gives you angst? Which makes your heart smile? Which makes you literally smile?

4. Ask the universe for guidance and direction by giving you a clear sign.

5. Let it go and wait.

The last step is important. No matter what, you must let it go. Remain objective; mentally walk away from it. Resist any temptation to deconstruct it, analyze it, or weigh in. Your gut is not interested in your opinion at this point. Whether you want to believe it or not, your intuition will always do right by you. As long as you keep your opinion to yourself, your gut will never fail you.

As I usually did, I wanted to see if the messages I lived by were around. *Please send me a message,* I said. *Guide me so that I can live my highest purpose.* After putting it out there, I went about my day. Exercise, of course, had long become a vital ingredient in my life. More than a vehicle through which to maintain my health, it was also another way of centering myself. After work that evening, I went downstairs to my basement gym and opted for a twenty-minute-long cycling class with one of the Peloton instructors I didn't often have the chance to follow.

I was glad. While I loved all the instructors, this one was known to be particularly excellent. Once she was ready, the class started out like any other. Then, after giving us a few words of inspiration, she touched on her own personal story. Before becoming a Peloton instructor, she said, she used to be a suit-wearing, high-powered financial analyst.

I looked up at the screen.

It was as if she had heard me put my question to the universe that morning. I kept pedaling and listened. Even though her friends, she continued, all told her she was crazy, she didn't think twice. She knew that helping people with their physical fitness was her life's purpose.

As she spoke, the soft glow on her face told me she was someone whose subconscious had experienced that expansive feeling—the one that comes when you're aligned with your purpose. Not only was she happy, she was at peace. In that instant, I knew I had just gotten my message. *Step aside, fear, this book is going to happen.*

Whenever you feel anxious or worried about going ahead with something, ask yourself what it is that stops you most of the time. You know the answer. It's fear. No doubt, you're already familiar with the popular acronym FEAR that helps drive home the point. I'm happy to share my own definition:

Fiction Emerging As Reality

If it helps you to invent your own acronym to make it stick, do it, because I promise you this: When you allow fear to retreat, you automatically make room for excitement to flow into your subconscious with pure abundance. That's when the magic and miracles really begin. And there is no bigger rush than that.

TUNING IN TO YOUR MESSAGES

Do you sometimes feel that you're alone in this world? That you're the only one on life's rollercoaster ride of challenges? Even with a network of family and friends, we've all been there at some point.

The thing is, we're never really alone. I believe that the universe sends us messages all the time as if it were a radio station. While the essence of each message varies, once you know how to access this station, you'll find the chatter on the airwaves to be pretty loud and clear. Sometimes the messages come to reassure us. Sometimes, to remind us. Other times, to warn us. Our task, then, is to tune into that frequency and pay attention.

• • •

Back to my cancer journey.

You may remember my telling you that when I received my first diagnosis (stage zero at age forty-two), requiring me to have a mastectomy, I changed nothing about my life—not my diet, not my relationships, not my outlook on life.

As a result, two years later the universe said, *OK, then. Knock, knock, Stacey. We thought we'd give you a little whisper in the ear the last time. Not something to kill you, of course, but something to scare you enough so you'd clean up your act. But you didn't listen. So now we're really gonna get your attention by giving you almost stage four.*

That, dear friends, is how the universe can call you out sometimes when you're not listening.

Oh, cr*p. They weren't kidding.

It was game over for me. I turned my approach upside down by spring-cleaning every corner of my life, this time "going public" with this second diagnosis. I even told the human resources department at my company to let me know if any employee needed help quietly.

"Put me on your list," I told them. "I'll be part of their support network if they want me. No one has to go through cancer or any other health challenge alone. I want them to know that they're going to have support through this."

The result? An outpouring of appreciation. That's when the magic unfolded. That's when I really began to feel expansive and see what was possible for my life. As if to reinforce this feeling, the universe sent me a message just days before my first chemotherapy session.

It was a Saturday, and my mom and I had made plans to go shopping for clothes, something we had often done in the past. This shopping day would not be our usual fun outing, however. This time, we were on the hunt for some sweats and other such items that would allow the doctors easy access to the port that had been placed in my chest for the chemotherapy. Despite my attempts to keep a smile on my face, there was a discernible heaviness in the air as we made our way to the mall. The doctor had said they were going to throw everything they had at the cancer. I was grateful. But inside, the big question kept coming: *Was I going to be OK?*

After arriving at the mall and parking, we began making our way to the entrance, when we saw it. Written in chalk on the ground at the top of three consecutive parking spots was a message I know in my heart was sent for me:

NEW BEGINNINGS

HAPPINESS

LOVE

My mom and I looked at each other as tears filled my eyes. Message received. Everything was going to be all right.

• • •

A similar experience happened to an acquaintance of mine.

Jillian, who came to a crossroads in her marriage in the middle of the pandemic, had returned to her hometown for two weeks to spend her birthday with her parents, but also to catch her breath and reconnect with her roots. She needed to take a pause before taking that next step. She was sure she was making the right decision. And yet she was hesitating. Why? She already knew the answer. It was fear.

One day, an old friend reached out to her after hearing that she was in town. Jillian remembered smiling as images of them as young girls swept through her like a soft breeze. The last time she had spoken to her childhood friend, the biggest concern they might have had was passing their final exams or trying to slip clear nail polish past the nuns at their all-girls Catholic school. How things had changed.

The following day, Jillian arrived at the outdoor bistro they had chosen for their rendezvous and saw her friend at a table, the smile on her face radiating a sense of inner peace. After exchanging a safe pandemic-style air embrace with a laugh, they sat. That's when her friend produced a small box from her tote bag.

"Happy birthday, Jilly," she said with a song in her voice. "We haven't seen each other in decades, so I don't know what you like or don't like, but for some reason I felt that this was right for you."

Jillian opened the box and pulled out the sheets of white tissue paper that enveloped her gift. When she pulled it out, she smiled. It was a glass coffee mug. Written in gold lettering were two words that she needed to hear: *Be Bold.*

TAPPING INTO YOUR SUBCONSCIOUS

First, a quick reminder of what our subconscious is: It's the part of our mind that we're usually not aware of, but which nevertheless influences our thoughts and decisions. The key word here, of course, is *aware.* In order to recognize the messages coming our way, we first need to become an observer of our mind and body.

Give it a try right now.

Look at yourself as if you were someone else and observe objectively. See what you're wearing. See how you're sitting or standing. Observe the expression on your face and how you're breathing. Then, focus. While everyone is different, I access my subconscious through the following process:

1. Let your mind go quiet. (While this is not easy to do, you can get there with practice.)

2. Once centered, ask the question: "Am I aware?" (It may sound silly, but this helps to state your intentions.)

3. Ask for a sign that only you would understand.

4. Let it go and wait.

Message watching has become such a fun part of my life that it has almost become a private game for me. Why not start this today?

Tell yourself that you're going to be open to receiving messages from the universe. The best part is you can play anytime and anywhere, as if turning the dial to your own private radio station. But remember, you have to stay tuned.

BLUE TURTLES ARE EVERYWHERE

Every year, I take my daughter, Sabrina, for a weekend to the New Jersey shore. It's a special girls' weekend we design for ourselves with no rules: We eat what we want, play as we wish, and do whatever makes us happy. There are no expectations other than to enjoy each other's company and have fun.

On our trip in 2020, the first year of the coronavirus pandemic, I took along a book I was reading called *Signs* by Laura Lynne Jackson. It's an impactful work about people who have passed on, and one I highly recommend for those who have lost someone close. As you probably guessed, it tells us that there are indeed signs everywhere showing that our loved ones are still talking to us. We just have to pay attention. And isn't that thought simply beautiful?

That first weekend morning in Spring Lake, I woke up in our Victorian beachside hotel to a majestic sunrise. With my daughter still sleeping quietly, I picked up my book, found where the bookmark was sticking out, and continued reading. After a few minutes, however, I put the book down. It was everything I believed. This time, I was going to put it to a really tough test.

OK, universe. If this is real, if the whole thing is real, I want you to show me a sign. But I want something so specific this time that it will leave no room for doubt. Show me a blue turtle.

And in case you're wondering, no, there was no significance to the blue turtle request. It was merely the first random thing that popped into my mind. And with that, I forgot about it and continued reading. Sometime after, my daughter woke up.

"Good morning, cutie pie. Where do you want to go for breakfast?" I asked with a smile, eager to start our mother-daughter day.

She shrugged as she stretched. "Oh, I don't really care," she said. "Maybe that place we saw yesterday. What's it called? A.M. Kitchen?"

By the time we arrived, a few patrons were already enjoying their morning meals, the clanking of cutlery and lively conversation filling the air. The host greeted us seconds later with a warm smile. But as the pandemic was still very much an issue, we were not comfortable with where he wanted to seat us. It was just a little too close to the neighboring table.

When I expressed my concern, he pointed to another table that was still occupied. Sitting under a tent off to one side, it was perfect. Our host said that if we didn't mind waiting just a few minutes longer, he would have it ready for us. The guests, he said, were already in the middle of paying their bill. We happily agreed to wait. Meanwhile, we entertained ourselves by taking in the eclectic decor. From where we stood, we could see that each table was decorated differently.

"Now that's a wonderful touch," I said to Sabrina. "I wonder how ours will look."

Minutes later we were seated. We started looking through the menus already set down on the table for us. With the large menus in our hands, the surface of our table was more clearly visible. That's when I noticed that ours was embellished with the most amazing mosaic in hues of blue.

I was about to return to reading the menu, when something caught my eye. *No, it can't be.* I leaned back for a better view. What do you think I saw? You got it—blended into the mosaic was a blue turtle. *That's it. Now I know that this stuff is real. No one can tell me otherwise.* Goose bumps, right?

Today, I wear a blue turtle necklace to remind me of that moment and just how powerful we really are.

MAKING IT YOUR PRIVATE CHANNEL

There have been other similar moments that assure me the universe is constantly sending us messages. Always talking to us.

A few months ago, after several years of keeping an eye on a suspicious freckle above my lip, I finally had it removed and biopsied. My mom, of course, was with me the day of the procedure, as she's always been whenever I need some unconditional love and support.

The freckle now gone, all that remained was the tortuous wait. As we left the doctor's office that day, we stopped by the Trader Joe's around the corner for a little distraction, and also because it's pretty much impossible to walk past a Trader Joe's without walking inside. Under normal circumstances, I might have gone straight home, not wishing to be out in public with a massive bandage on my face. But with the pandemic making us all wear masks, I looked like everyone else.

Less than a minute later, I came across two women in the aisle talking. That's when I overheard one saying, "No, they didn't find any cancer. It's benign."

I stopped, literally looked up above me, and whispered, "Thank you. Now I don't have to wait." In this case, I had not asked for a sign, but my focus was already on those pending results. A week later, they came in: no cancer.

I know you've already felt the wonder of communicating with the universe. You've had the experience, I'm sure, of thinking about someone you've not spoken to in ages, only to have them call you "out of the blue." Do you really think it's a coincidence? Energy is real. Remember, the universe is listening. Think of it as your private channel. All you need to do is tune in with intention.

One day in 2021, as summer was giving us its final few days of wonderfully balmy weather, I was home alone sitting on the couch, the steam from the hot mug of coffee in my hands slowly wafting under my nose. During moments like these, when I am alone and the world around me is still, I can almost touch the quiet happiness in my heart. This time was no different. Before long, my mind turned to my dad. Not a day had gone by since his passing when I didn't miss him. I would have done anything to see him or hear his voice again just one more time. I knew that nothing, not even the love of a daughter, could make that happen. But on that particular day, the little girl in me didn't care about what was realistic. She just wanted to be with her dad, if even for a few moments.

"Dad," I said, "if you're here, let me know."

All of a sudden, I heard a ringing in the near distance. It was a set of wind chimes that had been given to me as a gift in his honor. And in case you were wondering, no, it was not a breezy day. Even today, through the power of messages, my dad and I continue to have our father-daughter moments.

I mentioned earlier that exercising used to be an activity we loved to share together. One day while in my home gym, I decided to challenge myself to the thirty-minute endurance setting on the treadmill. While I loved exercising and fitness, running had never been a favorite activity of mine. After twenty-one minutes, I had to stop. The next day, my competitive side kicked in. "That's it," I said, "I'm going to do this." I started running and running. Suddenly, at the nineteen-minute mark, the machine completely shut down on its own. That had never happened before. I checked everything. Then I knew. Playing little harmless pranks like that was something my dad used to love to do. "Really, Dad?" I said with a chuckle.

The mind-universe connection is an awesome powerhouse waiting to be used. Trust it. Listen to it. Then let go and let the magic come your way.

OF CIRCLES AND SQUARES

As is the case with communication between people, we run the risk of misunderstanding what the universe is trying to tell us. This tends to happen when we are fixated on a certain goal or have certain expectations about how things are supposed to unfold for us. All we can see is that things are not going "according to plan." In fact, the universe is trying to send us an important message: You are exactly where you are meant to be. This is why listening to your gut and opening your mind to receiving messages is key. It's like I said before: Sometimes free will gets in the way.

I'll share with you a favorite story of mine that always fills me with gratitude and wonder.

In the time leading up to my divorce, I was desperate to find a town house for myself. I didn't want to rent it—I wanted to own it. In fact, I had already found a new development that was simply perfect. Day after day, I'd drive by the complex picturing myself hanging my pictures, putting up my blinds, and making my morning coffee. That was my plan, and I would stop at nothing to make it happen.

Every now and then, however, along comes what I like to call a circle-and-square moment. Do you know those geometric toys toddlers sometimes play with? I was pretty bad at that game, even as a child. I was always trying to force the circle into the square, despite my mother's constant warning.

"You'll break it if you keep doing that, Stacey!"

But I'd do it anyway.

This time, the challenge was the down payment. I didn't actually have it. My type A personality, however, wasn't taking no for an answer. After having spent a lifetime squeezing circles into squares to the point where they'd break, I wasn't deterred. *Bring out the broom and dustpan—this is going to happen!*

I tried everything. When nothing appeared to be working, I even went to the head of the town house community to see if there was a clause that permitted a purchase without a deposit. *Good try, Stacey.* I had not yet learned the important lesson that we should never try to force circles into squares, even with things meant for us. In the long run, it never quite works out.

Eventually, I got the message. That June, I signed a year-to-year rental agreement on an adorable place and moved in once I was free to do so. Exactly two months later, I met the man who would become my forever husband. (More on this in Chapter 8.)

Everything about him and us fell perfectly into place, including our living arrangements. Also recently divorced, he, too, was renting a place. As for his lease, it was up—you guessed it—in June. This meant that we didn't have to wait to sell anything when both of our leases were up. All we needed to do was find a place together and move in. Two years later, that's exactly what we did.

That's when it really hit me: All along, each blocked attempt to buy a town house was really the universe's way of sending me a message, but because I kept putting ego in the driver's seat, I couldn't see it. I was too intent on getting to my destination. The universe was trying to say, "No, not now, Stacey. Hear our message."

Since then, I have lived by a new rule that's been a game-changer for me: If the push starts to feel like a shove—like something is being forced to fit—then I know it's not meant to be, at least not this way and not this time. Today, I apply this approach to all situations, big or small. If I am turned down for a job that I know I'm qualified for, I accept that it wasn't for me. If I try to buy a pair of shoes that are out of stock, I let it go instead of hunting them down from store to store. Now I accept that this is the universe's way of talking to me.

This is not to say that you should give up after your first attempt. By all means, try, and even try again. We applaud spunk and determination. Just be sure to remain aware of how the process feels. Watch for that fine line between showing enthusiasm for a goal and noticing when you're forcing it. This is why trusting your gut is so important. It will tell you when something's off.

More importantly, have faith that all will be well. Trust that you will get to your destination. You may not get there in the direct line you had mapped out for yourself, but that's life. Don't give in to disappointment. See life as a road trip. Sometimes, for reasons we may not initially understand, we will have to stop and take a break. Sometimes it will take us on a more circuitous route than planned. And that's OK.

One way or another, you will find your way.

• • •

You are never alone. Never.

Messages are there to help you, and they are everywhere. You just have to be willing to receive them. Whether it's a song on the radio, the comment of a passing stranger—whatever it may be—know that the universe is constantly speaking to you. Tune in and listen carefully. This power—this connection—is already within you. All you need to do is engage it.

CHAPTER 4: KEY REMINDERS

- Whether you want to believe it or not, your intuition will always do right by you. As long as you keep your opinion to yourself, your gut will never fail you.

- We're never really alone. The universe is like a radio station sending us messages. Sometimes the messages come to reassure us. Sometimes, to remind us. Other times, to warn us. Our task, then, is to tune into that frequency and pay attention.

- There are blue turtles everywhere.

- Pay attention to those circles-and-squares moments: If the push starts to feel like a shove–like something is being forced to fit–then consider that perhaps it is not meant to be, at least not this way and not this time.

5

♥

DECONSTRUCTING
FEAR

When I think back to the days and weeks after filing for my divorce, the battle signs of cancer still visible as I signed the papers, I sometimes have to ask myself where *that* Stacey came from.

Did I really do that? While standing up to cancer?

Even today, each time I see myself in that moment, I feel a certain surge of unconditional love for myself I wish I could bottle and take as my daily multivitamin. If only it were that simple.

It was, in many ways, a turning of the corner for me. It didn't happen overnight, though. Long before I was even diagnosed, I sometimes dared to peek quietly at an image that I was secretly holding in my mind—one of life with a partner who was aligned with me, and a life that was overflowing with peace and happiness. I think that, even on my bleakest of days, something inside kept screaming at me to make my heartbeats count. *Stop throwing us away, Stacey!*

I like to think that it was the voice of that undeniable life force many of us have buried deep within us, the one that tells us what we need, if only we would trust it and listen. Mine was clamoring for a taste of joy. I wanted to get to a place where I was no longer settling for anything less than I deserved, a place where fear was rare, fleeting, and always low on gas. But after allowing almost my entire life up to this point to be driven by this near-crippling emotion, I was the one who was running on empty.

As I took those first small steps to healing my soul, I began to understand that, with every heartbeat, we build our life one moment at a time. I now saw that the choice was ultimately ours: We could view life as an event we simply attend or a party where we kick off our shoes and dance until our legs can no longer move. It was like opening my eyes for the very first time.

Since then, I wake up every morning imagining that I have just been handed a fresh juice box. After thanking the universe for one more chance to fill my soul with joy, I focus on my day with intention: to suck every drop of juice until that box is bone-dry. I know that if I'm lucky, I will get handed another box the day after. And the day after that. This is how I now live my life—one juice box at a time.

TAKING SMALL STEPS

While I was still in my first marriage and navigating the waters of what was clearly a turbulent situation, I didn't neglect myself completely, in case you were wondering. I did make attempts to heal. And as this was long before the cancer diagnosis, the healing I'm referring to here is that of the spiritual kind. The steps I took may have been small, but they were enough to loosen the jar lid on what had been, up to that point, a life with very little air or flow. This tends to happen when you live a fear-based life.

I remember attending this one seminar that had me taking my first real steps at shattering my fear-based belief system. Presented by a former boss-turned-friend back in 2005, the seminar focused on positive thinking and the practical ways in which to infuse this approach in one's life. One of her suggestions was to take fluorescent Post-it notes, write loving messages to yourself, and stick them where you'll see them daily. My notes went on my mirror. Each morning, as I brushed my hair, put on my makeup, and got ready for my day, I fed my subconscious these reminders:

- I am intelligent.

- I am strong.

- I am worthy.

- I am confident.

- I am powerful.

- I am blessed.

I'm sure you've probably already done this or something similar at some stage of your own journey. Did it work? How long did it take before you sensed a shift in your energy? And how long did its positive effects last?

I remember really getting into it, enjoying the role of observer, and sensing that I was aware of myself in terms of what I was thinking and doing, and the reasons behind them. I even began to use words like *strong* to describe how I was feeling. When those breakthrough moments of strength came, it was as if the window to the world of possibilities had cracked open ever so slightly, inviting me to break in and enter. Gradually, my incessant limited thinking disappeared, making way for an expansiveness that came over me like a wave rising out of the ocean. In those magical moments, I didn't just know I could do anything; I could feel it.

SHEDDING THAT SECURITY BLANKET

At first, I was able to hold on to this feeling only in snippets. I'd go through the day toggling as if I were two different people.

One minute I'd be all-in. Nothing and no one could stop me. And then, like a thief in the night, the tentacles of familiarity would return to grab me by the ankles and pull me back with barely a struggle. *And just where do you think you're going, missy?* That's when I'd scamper back to my little corner, with all my what-if fears welcoming me with open arms. I'd surrender to the life that I knew, one that had my soul aching—crying out for peace and joy. Once again, I was back to a fear-based life of limited thinking and sedated emotions.

Has this ever happened to you?

Have you ever gotten close to making that shift, only to allow fear to reel you back in by those chains only you can see?

It's frustrating, I know. But don't be hard on yourself. Changing years of conditioning takes more persistence and courage than you think.

You get to a happy place and think you're on solid ground. Then, suddenly, as if to test your mettle, your boss calls with a crazy rush assignment, a bill arrives with a wild error you now have to correct, and your toilet breaks down in your one-bedroom condo just as your plumber goes on vacation.

A sense of overload sets in. You panic. Suddenly, all you want is the comfort of something—anything—that is familiar. You want to be soothed by the feeling of a security blanket that's been worn and, let's admit, even a little less than fresh. I'm speaking as someone who once had such a blanket. I'll even confess that mine was downright filthy.

There is no shame in this.

Facing our fears is like waking up alone and shivering on a cold, gray morning. We know we should get up, but it's so much easier to just close our eyes and stay huddled under that familiar blanket.

Rest assured—you have lots of company. At some point, we have all been there. In fact, I think we all toe that line every single second of every day that we're trying to stretch ourselves. That's just part of challenging the status quo. When you're going through a serious transformation, however, the challenges can feel like you're trying to bench press your body weight for the first time.

Even those in our lives—including friends and family who love us—will expect us to act in a certain way or remain in a certain role because it's comfortable or convenient for them. When your decisions disrupt their comfort zones, they may try to push you back into the box.

What does this look like?

- They don't want you to move to another city for that dream job because they can't bear for you to leave.

Or:

- They don't want to see you with another partner if it means disrupting their social dynamics.

Steer yourself away from the temptation to sacrifice your happiness for the sake of others. If they truly care about you, they'll come around.

It's hard—I know.

From where you're standing, life may seem uncertain at best. But don't let fear paralyze you. Throw off that blanket, get up, and face the day. If you don't, you'll never see what's possible. If you can, stand back, look at yourself, and recognize that fear is whispering terrible nothings in your ear again. That's when you pull out your toolbox—the one with your name on it—and reach for whatever instrument it takes to tighten your resolve.

BREAKING THROUGH THOSE INVISIBLE BARRIERS

One gorgeous July afternoon, while in the middle of writing this book, I went for a quick power walk around my neighborhood. As the temperatures in the Northeast had been roasting us with plus-ninety-degree weather for days, the outdoors was the last place we wanted to be. So, when we finally had a break in the heat and humidity, I threw on my running shoes and headed out the front door.

That day, I chose to go down a road I had not yet explored. Walking at a fairly steady pace, I began turning my head left and right to look at the lovely houses, observing how each one told me something about the people that lived inside it. That's when I noticed him—a beautiful gray dog with a shiny coat in the yard of one of these homes. As I got closer, he began barking at me as if I was about to invade his doggie bowl. And then I saw his eyes. They were pools of warmth.

But in them I saw something else: fear.

I stopped where I was to take a closer look. Being a fur mom myself, I knew a bit about the language of dogs and wanted to allow him to check me out in a way that made him comfortable. If I sensed that he was OK with it, I would perhaps try to pet him on the head. At first, this beautiful creature took a few steps in my direction. But then, just like that, he halted, lowered his head as he took a step back, and gave a sad whine.

The smile left my face.

It was then that I noticed the advertisement sign for the company that had erected the security system with which to protect this beautiful animal. Suddenly, I understood. No matter how badly he wanted to venture out to connect with me and know what I was about, he would not. Not as long as there was a barrier that prevented him from expanding beyond where he stood. For those who don't know, this security feature sends a harmless shock to the animal's collar, deterring it from going past a set boundary invisible to the naked eye. And while in this case I understood that the fence was put up solely for his protection, I couldn't help but wince at the reminder that a fenced-in soul is all but a lifeless one.

• • •

We have a small white Maltese at home. Bella, who is no more than eight or nine pounds, rules our house, and we wouldn't have it any other way. Because she's so tiny, when she plays in our yard, we put a puppy bumper around her neck so she doesn't slip through the fence to an alternative universe where she would never be seen again. Bella has become so comfortable with this bumper that when we ask if she wants to go out, she immediately runs to it so one of us can put it on her.

While we are relieved that our fur baby understands the routine, what really struck me during her training period was that it didn't take long for her to condition herself to not go past a certain point. In fact, even if she didn't have the puppy bumper on, we are fairly certain that she would not even try.

The vision of both our neighbor's dog and our precious Bella really got me thinking about all our "invisible fences." You know what I mean—the mental barriers that stop us from embarking on the adventures or journeys we think are either too risky or beyond our capabilities. It might be the career we've always dreamed of, that promotion we want so badly, the trip of a lifetime we keep talking about, the romantic relationship we long to wake up to every day.

What stops us from reaching for our heart's desires? What tells us that we can't make these a part of our world? Our fears do. And each time we utter words of negativity, each time we add to that belief foundation, we drive yet another nail into our invisible fence.

What dreams are your mental bumpers or barriers stopping you from reaching?

And which fears are doing the talking?

- Fear of failure?

- Fear of being alone?

- Fear of judgment?

Fear, fear, fear. I lived for so many years with a mental barrier around me that when I look back to the person I was before this point, I almost don't recognize her.

Perhaps you're living behind one now. Tell yourself that you have lived there—*until now.* Think about it long and hard. The only person you have to answer to is you. You're capable. You're talented. You're intelligent. You're an amazing human being with so much to offer. The world is waiting for you to step into your glory. What are you really waiting for? If you don't think you can hop over that fence in one jump, then start chipping away at it daily. Before you know it, freedom will be but a heartbeat away.

JOHN'S FRESH START

Let's go back to the question posed to you in the opening pages of this book: How would you feel if you found out you had a potentially terminal illness? Intellectually, we all know that one day we will leave this life. But what if you got that sobering news today?

I recently heard about a man who, when told by his doctor that he had prostate cancer, experienced what he described as the most unexpected reaction. John said that after the initial shock wore off, a sensation came over him that he had not expected: a sudden calm. "Believe it or not, it was a feeling of complete liberation," he said. "It was as if I had been stripped of everything that had ever threatened to stop me from achieving a life of pure joy—all my worries, all the pressures of life, even the clothes I wore or the car I drove. It was as if I was facing the world naked. Suddenly, any fear or hesitation I had about anything completely vanished. I finally understood what it meant to feel free."

While he had always been a fairly upbeat person, for the first time, John could feel a lightness in his soul that had evaded him for most of his life. And it took a brush with mortality to get him there. The good news is that his doctor would go on to tell him in the next breath that the disease was curable—that while he would eventually die, it would not be from this disease unless left untreated.

On hearing the good news, John decided that he had just been given a chance to "refresh" his life as he did his computer screen when needed. It is a memory he returns to now and then whenever life tries to push his fear buttons.

As was the case with this individual, my health scare was the swift kick I needed. It's not that I would ever wish for it again (I don't), but having to face my greatest fear gave me the gift of freedom.

I was lucky. You don't want to—or have to—take it that far. You can start where you are right now. This is not to say I have it totally licked. I have my "moments." And when I do hear myself going down that road, my ears perk up. Now I'm aware enough to catch myself and strong enough to stop and say, *Yeah? And? Let's just move on to something else, shall we?*

I'm telling you now. Be aware of those energy-sucking, fearmongering thoughts. They are no longer welcome at my party. Don't let them into yours.

LILY'S LESSON

Another friend, Lily, recently shared with me a heartwarming story that serves as a reminder that we should always choose to have faith in what's possible.

Lily was your standard type A personality. She always paid her bills long before their due date, lived by daily to-do lists, and made sure her spices all faced forward in the pantry. She was also a self-admitted worrier. If she thought there could be potential landmines ahead, she would do whatever she could to clear them after first sorting them in alphabetical order. This meant that she was the kind of person who rarely misplaced or lost anything. That was her world. But when things did go wrong, her tendency was to immediately catastrophize and capitulate to fear. It was a crippling habit and unhealthy mindset she knew she had to correct.

One day, her sister asked her to accompany her on an impromptu business trip to Colombia. They had been to South America before but never to Colombia. Lily agreed to go, even though she would have preferred a bit more preparation time. The trip was coming up in less than a week and a half, and she had a lot on her plate.

"I immediately began talking myself out of the trip, coming up with all the reasons I couldn't go, including the pandemic, which was still not over. But my sister, who is my polar opposite, told me that I should just relax and come along for the ride and great coffee," said Lily. "So, I did."

From the moment the two landed in Cali, however, small details that would have made the trip a success all began slipping through the cracks. As if out of the pages of a novel, anything that could go wrong did. Hour after hour, the confusion compounded. Before they knew it, angst began to set in.

By the third day, it was clear that the short trip would have to be cut even shorter, and plans were made for a departure by day four. Both Lily and her sister were only too happy to go. The trip had morphed into a nightmare. On the evening of their last day, they arranged to have their COVID-19 tests done at their hotel, set their alarm for 2:45 a.m., and tried to get a few hours' sleep.

The next morning, they got ready quickly and hopped into the taxicab waiting for them outside the hotel lobby promptly at 3:30 a.m. When they pulled up to the airport forty-five minutes later for their 7:30 a.m. flight, the night sky still hovered. Groggy and in a haze from two sleepless nights in a row, the sisters thanked their driver in their best broken Spanish as they paid him. He smiled, gave them each an elbow bump, and wished them a safe flight. But just five minutes later while standing in line to check in, Lily's face went pale as she went to retrieve her phone from her pocket; it wasn't there.

She knew immediately what had happened: It had slid out of her pocket and onto the back seat of the taxicab. For a few seconds, she stood there picturing the phone disappearing forever into the city.

The phone itself, of course, wasn't the real problem. That could be replaced. Her and her sister's COVID-19 tests had been sent to them by WhatsApp. How were they going to board the flight? In that instant, Lily felt the panic rising fast as her heart seemed to jump to her throat.

This was classic Lily. She knew she was moments away from breaking into a cold sweat. But this time, instead of allowing fear to paralyze her, she forced herself to stop, take a few deep cleansing breaths, and embrace calm and logic. Then she began self-talking. *What can I do right now to fix this? There's got to be a way.* A few seconds later, it came to her. She took her sister's phone from her hands.

"What are you going to do?" her sister asked, the panic in her own voice now detectable.

"For once, I'm going to try having a little faith in what's possible. I'm going to call the nurse who administered our tests and ask him to send my certificate to your phone. I know it means asking him to bend the rules, but I have no choice. I've got to ask him." Her sister's eyes went wide.

"Bend the rules? That's hurdle number two. You need him to answer the phone first. It's barely four-thirty! Do you think he'll answer a call at this time of the morning? From a stranger?"

Lily nodded with half a smile as she took another deep breath. As she swapped her old mindset for this new and strange one, she felt her body reacting as an uncharacteristic calm settled in where anxiety once resided. Sensing a quiet confidence moving through her as she hit the "Dial" button, the only energy she put out into the universe at that point was hope, but hope without expectation. Even if the nurse didn't answer, she would have at least tried. And that first step felt good enough already. It was better than automatically declaring fear the victor by default.

"Know what?" Lily said. "Yes, I think he'll answer."

And he did. Less than an hour later, the two sisters were at the departure lounge, still in disbelief over what had just happened.

GOING FOR THE LONG SHOT

But the story didn't end there.

Lily decided to put faith to the test again by attempting to get her phone back. She admitted it was a long shot. She had left her brand-new smartphone in the back seat of a taxicab in a big city. Even if the driver was an honest person—and he did seem to be a decent man—it was entirely possible that he had already picked up his next fare.

Lily took another deep breath. Sitting there in the departure lounge, she allowed herself to focus only on the next logical step forward and not beyond that. Once she saw the result it produced, she would take the next step and the next. This was not like her at all. Lily had always been the kind who needed to see at least half the pathway to the end before making a move. It was a mindset she knew was unrealistic. At the end of the day, that's really all we have: the present moment.

Why, then, not take just one more step toward the positive?

Smiling again, she called the hotel and asked the front desk receptionist if he would do her the kind favor of contacting the taxi driver to ask if her phone was still in his car. And if it was, could he find a way to return it? After that first step, she let it go and got ready to board their flight.

By the time Lily and her sister landed in the States later that day, the hotel had reached out to say that they were already in possession of her phone. A week later, after a few more stars aligned thanks to the kindness of complete strangers, the phone was once again with its owner.

"When I set out to get it back, I honestly didn't know how it would play out," Lily told me. "But that feeling of letting faith take over gave me this quiet sense of hope that I will never forget. That's when a sudden lightness took over.

"There was no expectation, no sense of entitlement that it *had* to work out in my favor, which can often feel heavy and daunting. It was more a feeling of humility. I understood and accepted that anything could happen. That feeling of peace just flowed through me the entire time like a whisper. I'll never forget it. As for the people of Colombia, they will always have my gratitude and respect. It was as if they formed a human chain to pull me out of my little sinkhole."

The story, while admittedly a more superficial example of the power of a healthy mindset, reminded Lily that she needed to get into the habit of putting her trust into the possibility of a positive outcome, even when the odds are stacked against her.

THOUGHT TRACKER

Once she was back at home, Lily became curious. Just how often did she entertain negative thoughts? There was only one way to find out. She began to track them in a journal of sorts. There would be only three columns:

Day/Time:

Place/Situation:

Negative Thought:

At first, she was alarmed. She was averaging five paralyzing thoughts a week. *How did she become this person?* While she didn't have the answer, she knew that she had to find a way to turn this around. She told herself that each time she made an entry in her thought tracker, she would look at her mobile phone as a reminder of what was possible and ask herself three things:

1. How realistic was this fear?

2. What could she do to change its trajectory?

3. And if the situation she feared did materialize, how could she adapt to live with it?

Within two months of monitoring herself, Lily noticed a shift in her outlook. While her tendency to have fearful thoughts remained, they came less frequently and left her mind a lot faster than before. Now, situations that would have had her up at night in the past no longer had that potency. While she still had a lot of work to do, she felt proud of herself for taking even small steps to rein in that unhealthy habit. And while she admitted that she would always tend to be a worrywart, she had finally found herself an effective tool with which to keep it in check. And because of that, she said, life had become just a little bit easier.

• • •

Fear comes in so many forms. What gives one person anxiety is par for the course for another.

Know yourself and take action.

Lose sleep over your finances? Seek the help of a professional, or talk to a friend who's financially successful and good with numbers. They may have a perspective you can't see. Worried about your career? Talk to a headhunter or a friend who's risen through the ranks of a big company. Health issues? With your doctor's permission, join a gym. Short on funds at the moment? Go walking in your neighborhood or jog around your house. The point is, sometimes we need to stop and think about it, but when we do, we'll usually find that there is always a way.

Please. Get started on your journey to joy. Do whatever it takes to push fear as far away from you as possible. It's the only thing stopping you from living the life you deserve. Don't wait until you're on your last heartbeat.

CHAPTER 5: KEY REMINDERS

- Get to a place where you are no longer settling for anything less than you deserve–a place where fear is rare, fleeting, and always low on gas.

- Wake up every morning imagining that you have just been handed a fresh juice box. Decide that you're going to enjoy every drop of juice until that box is bone-dry. Live your life one juice box at a time.

- Have you ever gotten close to making that shift, only to allow fear to reel you back in by those chains only you can see? Don't be hard on yourself. Changing years of conditioning takes more persistency and courage than you think.

- A fenced-in soul is all but a lifeless one.

- What stops us from reaching for our heart's desires? What tells us that we can't make these a part of our world? Our fears do. And each time we utter words of negativity, each time we add to that belief foundation, we drive yet another nail into our invisible fence.

6

ADD GRATITUDE
AND STIR

Earlier on, I said I believe we are always where we are meant to be at any given moment. Stop and really think about this. Examine the spirit of the message: If you can see that every experience brings with it a valuable lesson, then you can't help but feel gratitude for whatever life sends your way. This holds true for everything, including the challenges we face in our journeys. Reading this book right now is part of your journey, just as the journey that became this book's foundation was part of mine.

If you're going through a tough time at the moment, hear me now: I know you're suffering. I know it's hard. You may even be in a situation where you have to take it one minute at a time. But if you can find something about your situation for which to be truly grateful, and if you can put your experiences to positive use, you *will* get through this. Let me say it again:

You *will* get through this.

Hold gratitude in your heart and watch as you evolve to become an even better version of yourself. Ask my daughter. She'll tell you that I've taught her to sift through her day, every day, and look for the gems among the rubble.

"Yes, OK, today kinda sucked," I'll say, "but what lesson did you learn?"

• • •

Viewing a rough patch in your day through a rose-colored prism is not easy, and probably not second nature, I'll give you that. I'll even concede that self-pity can feel deliciously soothing in the moment. (Directions: Squeeze out of a bottle like lotion and slather on at will.) Even the strongest among us will occasionally fall for its lure. But any immediate gratification we get from living with a victim mindset is short-lived. In fact, indulging in it is an act of self-defeat.

Do you suspect that you might reach for this mindset now and then? Or maybe a little too often? If so, have you ever peeked in the mirror to see how it really looks on you? If you can't bear to do this now, think of someone you know who fits the description. Picture that person right now. Notice their facial expressions—the dullness in their eyes and the tightness in their jaw. Notice the bitterness in their negative words. (And I want to make it clear that I am not talking about people who suffer from depression.)

Do you notice yourself taking a step back when in the presence of these individuals? You wonder why anyone would willingly hurt themselves this way. It almost looks like self-loathing—an aberration of nature.

They are like this because they haven't discovered the magic of the gratitude mindset, even though it's within their reach. These individuals, through no fault of their own, are stuck. They're living in the past. If they're stuck in the past, they're not in the present. And if they're not in the present, they're not living. Not really.

As so many of us do, they are allowing their inner child to rule the roost without even knowing it. What are they doing with their heartbeats? Are they spending them in ways that are helpful? While I defer to the mental health professionals who can help you with your inner-child discovery, I want to remind you that we are all works in progress where this is concerned.

What about you? Are you now becoming more aware of the choices you're making as you go about your day? Are you observing how you react to certain situations? Do you understand what's behind it?

The mind is not just any tool; it is *the* most powerful one you will ever own. And it's yours to use as you wish. Will you use it to help or hinder you? The choice is yours to make. What stories will you let your mind tell you about yourself or about a situation you find yourself in?

EASY DOES IT

Much has been written about ways in which to develop the gratitude mindset, with more and more people now talking openly about expressing gratitude in their daily lives. Journaling, of course, is a popular method through which to do this. But for those who don't enjoy journaling, here's a simple suggestion you may find effective. Limit yourself to one minute a day; then increase the time as you grow more comfortable. The point is not to force it but to start it:

1. Pick a daily activity you enjoy. This could be having that first cup of coffee or tea, exercising, standing under that warm shower, or even getting dressed for the day. If a daily commitment feels overwhelming, start weekly then build on it. Remember, you are developing a healthy habit. Eventually it should feel like joy, not work.

2. For one minute only, acknowledge just three things you're thankful for. If possible, say these out loud. Go as deep as you want ("I'm grateful I woke up this morning") or as playful ("I'm grateful I applied my eyeliner just right today").

3. If you're bashful about saying these out loud but still don't want to do traditional journaling, jot them down in your smartphone.

Be as quirky as you want about your secret minute of gratitude. I know someone who chose her minute while doing house chores that made her want to scream (e.g., cleaning the vacuum cleaner). The result? She changed her attitude about the chores she once found a nuisance. "It made me realize that I was grateful I had a house to clean," she said. "Once I got into the habit of being thankful for the little things, I began to stack my gratitude. Over time, I was able to view difficult situations with a level of grace I never had before."

There was another who spent her minute of being thankful each time she got into her car and slipped into the driver's seat. "I never forgot that there was a time when I didn't have a car that I could just jump into," she said. "Life had been good to me, and I needed to remember this."

And there was a third who would smile each time she was able to complete even a thirty-second-long plank. "Years before my back pain was so severe that I could barely walk. Suddenly, being able to do a plank seemed like a privilege."

$$\bullet \ \bullet \ \bullet$$

While I can't pinpoint exactly when I developed my own version of a gratitude mindset, I can only assume that it began in my childhood. Even though my family's struggles were plain to see, I think something in me never lost sight of the fact that we were still pretty lucky in so many ways. Somewhere in my young girl's heart, I believed that it would all work out. Today, I know that the challenges that came my way eventually brought out the best in me. And for this I am grateful.

As I go through some of the highlights of my personal story, think about your own memories. See if you can change the frowns they once caused into a smile. If you can find the lessons, I promise you will find the joy.

FROM WELFARE TO FARING WELL

There's one place in my memory where I could have walked in wearing a blindfold and earplugs and still have known where I was. In fact, I'm pretty sure I could do it even today. That signature smell never left me, the one of stale urine that always tickled my nostrils within twenty steps of walking through the door of our Bronx neighborhood social welfare office.

That's where my mother, sister, and I found ourselves every Tuesday afternoon after school, shuffling forward in a snaking line waiting to collect our food stamps, our eyes fixed ahead at the clerk's window at the top of the hall. The closer we got to our destination, the closer we were to our next TV dinner (my hands-down favorite was meatloaf with a side of vegetables and a brownie for dessert), or pizza if we felt we deserved to splurge, or Spanish rice and spareribs if Mom had the time to cook, which she rarely did.

But first, immediately following the procurement of those precious food stamps, we had the promise of fresh air beyond the building's glass doors, its metal handle across the middle worn smooth over the years from the hopeful hands that pushed it open.

I was, and still am, a proud Bronx kid, born and raised until the age of fifteen—time enough to set like Jell-O. But almost from the start, our little family proved unable to hold it together as a team. I was just two and a half years old when my parents divorced. When my father subsequently moved to Maine and remarried, my mother became the single parent of two young girls—my older sister, Deb, and me.

From that point on, home was a place called Co-Op City, a busy Bronx neighborhood that was a hub of ethnic diversity—a true melting pot that makes me feel lucky for having experienced it in my foundation years. Even today, I still smile whenever I flip through my old school pictures and see the different faces smiling back at me.

I'm sure that, for some, having this kind of hand-to-mouth existence would stir negative feelings. Even growing up in a concrete-bound environment may seem less than desirable. But I have nothing but gratitude for it. I view the experience as a reminder that every difficult situation has its blessings. As for our urban home, not only did I find it fun as a kid, I know without a doubt that Co-Op City's plucky energy helped to instill in me the fighting spirit that I would eventually draw on in my adulthood.

I'll go even further. While I may not have thought so at the time, I believe that growing up in the family that I did gave me a front-row seat to some of life's most important lessons. Take my courageous mother for instance. Determined to find her way in life as a single parent, she came off welfare by juggling two or three jobs at a time. During the day, she worked as a paraprofessional teacher, and after school sold photograph portrait packages door to door. And at night, she pursued her teaching degree at Lehman College.

For three or four years, our mom kept this difficult pace until she began to feel some financial traction under her feet. This meant that long before all my permanent teeth had come in, I was already learning what a truly strong woman really looked like, and not just in terms of work ethic. With the small ounce of energy that remained after taking care of all the essentials, she did what she could to lift herself up.

Our mom worked, set her financial goals, made personal goals, and kept a firm eye on both. Once she became a bilingual teacher at age thirty-two, she kept her teacher's hat on and immediately began showing her young daughters how to save, something that had been impossible to do while we were on welfare. Beyond teaching us that saving was not only for the rich, this healthy habit drove home the message that we should always have enough faith in life to look past our current challenges and hold in our vision a future of unlimited possibilities. How could I not be grateful for that?

The hard work now behind her, Mom allowed herself to revel in the new career she had visualized for her future, often joking that her students—mostly Hispanic at that time—were learning English with a perfect Bronx accent (*my muth-ah, my fath-ah, my sis-tah*). I remember watching her beam with joy and feeling so incredibly proud of her. She was so swept up by the Spanish language, that she would have Deb and me talk in Spanish at home for days at a time.

Looking back, I know that my mom understood the power of gratitude, even if she didn't know how to articulate it. She worked with what she had and took nothing for granted.

I didn't know it then, of course, but witnessing this young single mother take charge while still honoring her dreams was nothing short of a priceless gift to me, particularly as a daughter. By doing this, our mom taught us by example another valuable lesson: You should always put on your oxygen mask first before helping others. If you don't, you won't have the strength to elevate others—either physically or emotionally—no matter how much you want to.

This is why I view my parents' divorce with gratitude. While at the time my sister and I saw it differently, the fact was our parents were simply not what the other needed. They brought out the worst in each other and pushed each other's buttons. As much as every child wants to see their family remain intact, I shudder to imagine what would have happened had they stayed together. No doubt my sister and I would have been witnessing two people squandering their heartbeats in resentment, anger, and sadness. To see our parents make the decision to move on and find happiness was an example of bravery and courage; it was a gift that my sister and I would unwrap later in our own adult lives.

This is not to say that I blindly see everything through rose-colored glasses. I don't. What I try to do at all times is focus on the treasures I am able to find. For example, I still readily admit that, despite my father's efforts to remain in our lives, I have always struggled with abandonment issues. Just like the smell of the welfare office that never left me, that feeling of loss stalked me even up to a year or two before he passed away in 2020.

NO REGRETS

"Why did you have to move so far away, Dad? Why?"

I would ask him this question whenever the two of us—father and daughter—would go for walks on the beach, our pants rolled up to just above our ankles, shoes in our hands, the breeze carrying the sound of dogs barking playfully at their owners, who were also out for some fresh air. Like looking for that perfect seashell, I'd wait to feel the courage rise within me before asking these and other tough questions.

I remember my father once telling me, his voice low but steady, that since we can't rewrite the past, the most we can ask for is to be at peace with the decisions we have made. It was a message of self-love and forgiveness that I would use to soothe myself from time to time. Then he stopped and stared ahead at the ocean. That day, the tide was low under a cloudy sky. The Atlantic waves, usually moody along the Maine coast, eyed us cautiously from a distance. The sand, still damp from the retreating water, was ice-cold to our feet, but only at first. After a few minutes, our feet could no longer sense the sting they had initially felt.

"Cookie," my dad said, "if I could do it all over again, I'd have done it differently. It's one of my biggest regrets. But you need to know how much I love you."

In that moment, seeing my dad cloaked in his humanity, I felt nothing but unconditional love for him. For all the pain I had gone through up to this point in my life, I would not have traded a second of it if it meant not having this precious moment with him because I was sure of one thing: all our bumpy roads had led us to this moment. And for this, I was eternally grateful.

In my most honest of moments, I know that my parents' divorce blessed us with an important lesson: Just because you love someone, it doesn't mean you can live with them. My parents, well-intentioned high school sweethearts when they wed, were perhaps too young to understand the dynamics of a good union. They were, as it turned out, simply a perfect mismatch. Had they stayed together, it is entirely possible that I would still be in my first marriage, thinking that daily friction was a normal part of a relationship.

Because Ellen, my stepmother, knew how to stand up to my father, because she put him in his place when needed—and it was needed at times—she was able to build a better relationship with him. She was able to help him sort out his rough edges. As a result, theirs was a true partnership.

With each summer I spent with them, I got the chance to observe the anatomy of a strong union. I witnessed that natural easiness that comes when two people are confident—first in who they are as individuals, and second, in the relationship they share with each other. The air is simply that much lighter. You feel the energy of possibility. You hear the soft clicks of pieces falling into their natural place. It was an example I never forgot and one that would serve me well in the years to come.

ADDING A DASH OF COMPASSION

Ending a relationship is never easy. Even under the best of circumstances, it can tear at you in ways you can't imagine. But if you can see adversity as the gateway to self-knowledge—to knowing how you want to spend your heartbeats—you can't help but feel gratitude and its close cousin, compassion, for the situation—or the person—that led you to this point of your life. Just as pressure is needed to form diamonds, grapes are crushed to make wine, and seeds are buried in the damp and darkness, we find true transformation under uncomfortable circumstances. This is when the hero in us hears our call to break through and save us.

• • •

I can honestly say that I harbor no ill feelings toward my ex. For him I have only compassion and the sincere hope that he is able to find lasting joy.

Had he not come into my life to shine a light on the issues I needed to work on, I would not have found the impetus with which to begin my journey. I would not have found the courage to begin healing. I would not be in the process of becoming the butterfly that I know I am meant to be. And I would not have gone on to find the man who would become my forever life partner.

To make the point, and to show why I am truly grateful for the lessons I learned through my ex, I'll share with you a private conversation that took place between my mom and me around this very topic. One day while I was gathering my notes for this book, she asked me if I thought I would have been attracted to Ed before I became healthy. As much as I think the world of this man, I actually had to stop and think about it. I put the mirror up, which is always exhausting but important, and held it there until I could answer honestly.

"No," I eventually said. "The person I was then would have found him too kind. Too nice. The person I was then did not know what that was. I would not have recognized it. I would not have understood it."

The saying "water seeks its own level" is so true.

Whatever we are feeling about ourselves—whether good or bad—is what we are attracted to in others and, in turn, is what we attract. When I met and married Tom, I had low self-worth, and therefore attracted into my life what I thought I deserved. But the unhappier I became, the more I felt the need to change my life. That's when the disconnection between us began to grow. This happened as well with certain friends. Over time, I became aware of the fact that when I was with them, I was just going through the motions.

Have you ever had that unsettling feeling that there are those in your life with whom you are not aligned?

You're smiling on the outside, maybe even laughing, but it's more forced than felt. There is no sparkle in your eyes. Pay attention. Those are your heartbeats trying to tell you that something is off.

Every now and then, I take what I call my *Best-For* test. It's an exercise in which I force myself to question whether a certain person is best for me, even if they have been in my life for a long time. Give it a try. Take stock of whatever situation you're in. Notice where you

WHERE DO YOU SPEND YOUR HEARTBEATS?

spend your time and with whom. This is your journey and you're simply gathering information. Just remember to be honest with your answers. To begin, identify the person(s) causing you to have some doubt. Now ask yourself these questions:

BEST-FOR TEST

1. Do you still feel they bring out the best in who you are, or do you find yourself now feeling a bit agitated when in their company?

2. Do they seem interested in what you bring to a conversation, or do you sense that they're more interested in lining up their next response?

3. Do you find yourself wondering how soon you can make an exit, or does time seem to fly by when you're with them?

4. Do you feel like yourself when you're in their company, or do you notice that you hold back on certain aspects of your personality?

5. Do you feel energized about the things you talk about or generally uninspired?

6. Do you feel better about yourself when you leave them, or do you feel as if you could have spent your time more wisely?

There is no judgment, no shame. You're not saying that these are bad people. I don't believe that there is such a thing, to be honest. Instead, I believe that there are only people who are misaligned with you or better aligned with others.

• • •

Is there something in your life right now that's stirring angst in you? Know that you have the power to control even the most challenging of situations. Reach for that power by stepping into gratitude. Try it now. Use your heartbeats to flood your mind and heart with it and feel the fear and sadness melt away.

CHAPTER 6: KEY REMINDERS

- Any immediate gratification we get from living with a victim mindset is short-lived. In fact, indulging in it is an act of self-defeat.

- While your childhood may not have been ideal, try to see it as your time in a front-row seat to some of life's most important lessons.

- We should always have enough faith in life to look past our current challenges and hold in our vision a future of unlimited possibilities.

- Since we can't rewrite the past, the most we can ask for is to be at peace with the decisions we have made.

- If you can see adversity as the gateway to self-knowledge, to knowing where you want to spend your heartbeats, you can't help but feel gratitude and its close cousin, compassion, for the situation—or the person—that led you to this point of your life.

7

♥

THE POWER
OF WORDS

Raise your hand if you've ever gone on a diet to improve your health. I have a gazillion times. What is a diet anyway? It's a decision to make wise choices about the foods you put into your body. As I mentioned, during my cancer journey I had to learn the hard way that food can either hurt or help your body. When it comes to the words we think and speak, it's no different. Both can profoundly affect our mental health.

What words have you been putting out into the universe? Have you ever paid attention to how they land? What's the impact on those around you? And, more importantly, what's the impact on your mental and emotional well-being? Do you even know? Whether we realize it or not, the quality of our lives—if not the very creation of it—lies in the power of our tongue.

"CANCEL, CANCEL!"

Once I started to get healthy—mind, body, and spirit—I began to take note of many everyday expressions that, in my mind, felt at odds with my new outlook. *How interesting that we say things that don't actually serve us well.*

After a while, I stopped using some that I felt did not support my personal journey. While they seemed harmless enough, I felt that the essence of their message was too negative for my new path. And after having brought myself back from my life's lowest ebb, I wanted to stand guard at the gateway of my mind and soul.

Today, I avoid using these and other phrases. And if I do slip and allow them to fly out of my mouth, I immediately say, "Cancel, cancel!"

The new Stacey makes it a point to avoid saying things like, *I'm sick of.* This—no surprise—was the first expression that went on my "Cancel, Cancel!" list. After having battled cancer, I wanted no more talk of being sick, period. Others included *Give me a break.* Who wants a broken limb? Ouch! Then there's the ever-common *I'm fed up.* That's too close to home for me because of weight gain. And you can guess how I feel about *It's to die for.* Nope, I'm not saying that either. Then there are some of the harshest things one can say: *would've, could've, should've.*

AVOIDING THE REGRET RABBIT HOLE

This last group is akin to curse words in my vocabulary.

Sometimes they still slip out of my mouth or enter my mind. Sometimes I'll even say them in a crowded room. Each time I utter these words of regret, I know I am wasting my heartbeats. I honestly feel that I am crushing my very soul. This is why I put a loud and bright note on my desk to remind me how such thoughts can send me spiraling into trouble.

I don't exaggerate when I use the word *trouble.* If you've never gone down the regret rabbit hole, kudos to you for being strong. It is an experience you want to avoid at all costs. Those who have fallen into it will tell you that it is an abyss that has the power to siphon every ounce of joy out of you. If you're not careful, if you don't monitor those words and thoughts of regret, you run the risk of falling into a deep depression. Once there, it takes every ounce of strength and self-love to climb your way out of it.

Think about it: When you do venture to Yesterville—because we all do that now and then—do you merely pass through to say "Hi" and then leave? Or do you unpack your bags and settle in to stay? How much time do you really spend thinking about the things you would have done, could have done, should have done, if only (insert regretful thought here)? Be honest.

- A couple of times a year?
- A few times a month?
- Weekly?
- Daily?

I know someone who made the mistake of looking at her biggest regrets as she approached middle age. What started out as a quick glance in the rearview mirror ended up being a sojourn that had troubling consequences. Because her words and thoughts of regret went unabated, she fell into depression that lasted for months. It was, in her words, one of the bleakest times of her life.

"When I look back at that self-inflicted wound, I can't help but shake my head at the irony. There I was wasting my time and energy lamenting over the time and energy I had wasted decades before."

Please. If you care about your well-being, don't go near the rabbit hole of regret, no matter how low you're feeling. In fact, erect a wall around it and stick a huge "Do Not Enter" sign next to it.

Be kind. Tell yourself the truth: There is no wrong action. Always remember that you are, at all times, exactly where you are supposed to be, learning exactly what you are supposed to learn.

When I look back on my life, I know that everything unfolded in the exact sequence necessary for me to become the person I am today.

THE TALES WE TELL OURSELVES

With every word, we create our reality. This is especially true of the words we tell ourselves quietly. This is why I make myself accountable for what I'm thinking. I write down my thoughts, read them, then ask myself if this is how I would speak to a loved one. Are these thoughts kind? Or is this a story I'm telling myself? Because we tell ourselves stories all the time, most of them false.

Did you ever have a friend not call you when they said they would, only to have you wrap an entire story around why they didn't? You wonder if it's because of something you said in your last conversation, and now they're angry with you. That's a story. And then you find out that they temporarily misplaced their phone, so they couldn't call. *Boom!* It wasn't about you.

On my birthday in October 2021, I ended up spinning a work of fiction worthy of a Pulitzer. As a treat to myself, I had taken the day off from work that Monday. After sleeping in a little, I woke up the way some of us birthday junkies do—with a smile and a great big stretch. After all, it was my special day, and it was going to be magnificent. But there was more. After the major health challenge I had faced, the privilege of being able to celebrate another year of life had come to mean even more to me. I got dressed and made myself an amazing cup of coffee.

By this point, I had received a few calls from some of my early-bird family and friends, and was I happy. Eventually, I jumped on the computer to check my email and social media. But instead of seeing the magnificent fountain of love I had come to look forward to over the years, I saw a light trickling. I had received literally a couple of emails, but little else. *Huh?*

Meanwhile, the doorbell remained quiet. Not a delivery, card, treat, flower or bow in sight. Honestly, I felt my shoulders drop with each minute that passed. Without skipping a beat, I let my mind take over: *Stacey, you suck.* I did say that I'm still a work in progress, right?

Before long, however, the puzzle was solved: The big social media platforms had gone offline that same morning, which resulted in most of my birthday messages being delayed by a day. By Wednesday, our house was filled with flowers and gifts that had arrived late due to the supply chain issues being felt across the board. My mom and husband couldn't stop laughing—at me.

"Stacey," Ed asked, "did you really think that everyone suddenly stopped loving you overnight for no reason?"

My face went tomato red.

After the laughter subsided, I asked them both what lessons they thought I had just received as my bonus birthday gifts. Ed said I had been reminded that I do not need external validation. My mom said that I should always have faith.

What nonsensical stories have you told yourself? Pay attention to them the next time you hear one beginning to unfold.

WATCHING WORDS IN ACTION

Stories aside, have you ever listened to how you speak to or about yourself in general? Some time ago, a friend of mine shared a story about observing the power of words in action. It was such an everyday example, Cathy said, that she almost missed it. After all, she had seen many before that were much more extreme, some even bordering on the morose. But this example, on this day, really resonated. And for that, she was grateful.

CATHY'S STORY

Cathy, having a free morning one Saturday, decided to visit a friend at his newly opened ballroom dance studio. Not only did he want Cathy to see his new venture, he wanted her opinion on his progress with one particular student who was having extreme self-confidence issues. Her name was Melissa. To her credit, taking dance lessons was Melissa's attempt to challenge herself and build her self-esteem. As a gentle start, she decided to go with private classes.

Her instincts were spot-on. Learning a new sport or physical activity was a fantastic idea. After all, motion improves our emotion. In addition, when we conquer any new skill, especially one we consider to be difficult, we automatically experience a boost of confidence that helps us face other challenges.

Maybe you've also tried this hack. No doubt it helped. But did you stay in that place of awareness? Did you support it with your words? As simple as it sounds, it's important to treat yourself with kindness, even when just trying out a new hobby. It was something that Melissa had forgotten.

Cathy arrived at the studio that morning just as the class was about to begin. As she settled into her chair, she waved to her friend and Melissa, who were both on the dance floor. But literally within minutes of starting, Melissa began to use phrases that had the effect of nails screeching against a chalkboard:

"I don't feel comfortable."

"I don't like this."

"It's too hard."

"I'll never be good at this."

"I look ridiculous."

Then there was the one she had on repeat for almost the entire hour: "I can't do this."

Cathy sat up, her heart racing a little. She put the mirror up to herself. She couldn't deny it. Once upon a time, these were words she would have used without even thinking. Honestly, it felt like an attack against the soul. Is this the aura she once emitted when she engaged in the language of lack? Did she look this unhappy in the eyes of others?

Cathy wanted to give the student, almost twenty years her junior, some encouragement so she began cheering her on. It seemed to help. But there was a twist. At the end of the class, Melissa smiled and turned to Cathy.

"And what about you? How about giving it a try?"

Cathy, who herself was a recovering negativity addict, admitted that her former first instinct—to decline immediately—tried hard to push its way past her now-panicked smile. As she sat there, the music still floating through the speakers, she heard the excuses secretly queuing up in her mind:

I only came to observe.

I'm not wearing the right shoes.

I couldn't buy a rhythm if it were on sale.

But then Cathy caught herself. She was not going to give in to fear. *Heck, yeah!* She jumped up from her chair and made her way to the dance floor. Ten minutes later, she had managed to learn the basic step.

THE ANATOMY OF FEELING EXPANSIVE

How did Cathy make this shift? How did she coax herself into giving an emphatic *yes*? She shared the details of that moment with me when we met for coffee days later.

"Right there on the spot," Cathy said, "I had a quick private chat with the inner me that was shaking a little in her sneakers. I told myself that I was in control of this moment. The choice was mine. It was the feeling of consciously choosing an expansive feeling and turning it into action. Before I could talk myself out of it, I said *yes*, kicked off my shoes, and jumped out of that chair.

"To push the envelope," she continued, "I pictured myself doing well. But I also did something else: I let it go. I consciously removed all expectations of a desired outcome. I did not tell myself that I had to do well or else. I did not make any demands of myself. I took that off the table. That adjustment, I think, made all the difference. It was like lifting the valve off a pressure cooker. If I aced it on the first try, fantastic. If it didn't happen, I'd accept that, too, and with a full heart. Honestly, it felt like an act of self-love.

"The result? Even before I got on the dance floor, a new kind of peace came over me. I felt unlimited—as if I had stepped through a portal into another realm where anything was possible. And then I did it. Let me tell you—it was like having stardust sprinkle down on me. The experience set the tone for my entire day and week.

"I now use this most recent experience as a tool when I need a little nudge to try something new. I'll be the first to admit that I am still struggling with this, but I like to think that I was able to see Melissa's example clearly because I'm now healthier. I have to tell you, it was jarring. I still shudder to think that I used to be like that."

WORD BY WORD

We all experience doubt. Even those of us who seem to be brimming with confidence have our moments. The trick is to use words and thoughts that support you. Fake it if you have to. Tell yourself that you can get to the other side of whatever challenging situation you're in. See it. Feel it. Then go for it.

Deep down, most of us are hungry for words of encouragement. Even if we are considered experts at what we do, we still react with genuine appreciation when someone takes the time to support us.

I like to believe we are all positive thinkers and motivators in training; some of us are simply more advanced than others. What about you? Do you have more work to do in this area? For those just starting out, try building a list of default positive responses to both people and situations. Even if the appropriate response should include words of caution, always start with a happy spin and add a smile if you can. Word by word, you can give others the lift they need.

DEFAULT POSITIVE RESPONSES

1. "Good for you! I know you're scared about the late acceptance to that program, but you're going to give it your all."

2. "Congratulations! It sounds like a challenge you're going to enjoy and conquer."

3. "I think you're going to be just fine. I can tell you're determined."

4. "You're strong, smart, and talented. You're going to do well."

When you're the subject of the conversation, be ready to present yourself in the best light possible while being truthful:

5. "My superpowers lie elsewhere. I'm a natural at analytical thinking." (Say this with a confident smile.)

6. "Thank you!" (When paid a compliment, always accept it.)
"It took some work but I love the outcome as well."

YES!

Have you ever noticed the effect the word *no* has on you?

Depending on the context, of course (because sometimes *no* is the right answer), it can make you cringe a little. In my two-pronged healing journey—from cancer and from emotional pain—I began to enjoy the popular trend of having *Yes Days*. These were days when I would promise myself to do things that scared me—things that I would have said no to in the past.

Starting soon after my divorce, I began joining meetup groups for activities that the old Stacey would have normally been hesitant to try. I'd tell myself that, just for that day, as long as the activity wasn't illegal, immoral, or dangerous, I would say yes. Sometimes I'd end up driving by myself for hours away from home to go hiking with strangers. Not only was it exhilarating, I met some pretty special people, some of whom are still in my life.

Each time I did this, I found my mind opening up to what was possible. After living a life with a limited mindset, it was a refreshing change. Over time, I began to see myself transforming, not just in what I was doing but in how I was thinking and feeling.

After a while, I added another approach called my *No Should Days*.

Those days revolve around my love and need for structure. (Yes, I'm a type A.) Watching what I eat, working out, and doing what keeps me healthy always makes me feel good. That said, I'm also wonderfully human. Sometimes, I just need to have a day with a judgment-free spirit and no rules governing what I should and should not do. That's when I'll say yes to mimosas and ice cream for breakfast, yes to going out in my pajamas, and yes to just letting go. My *Yes Days* and *No*

Should Days are to my mind and soul what my green juices are to my body.

Why *do* we say no? What's really behind it? For 2021's Memorial Day weekend, I ended up having a magnificent impromptu *Yes Day* with my daughter that got me to wondering about this question.

YES WEEKEND

Things in the United States were just beginning to open up once again at about that time. Because I had been vaccinated (no judgment either way), I felt a little more comfortable making plans safely, and I began filling up my calendar as much as I could. But for some reason, that weekend was clear. It felt weird but good. My daughter had gone into Manhattan to meet up with friends for brunch, while my husband was away with his kids enjoying their time together.

As a result, the house was quiet. So, I said to myself, *Self, you don't have any plans this weekend, and no expectations. Isn't that wonderful? Let's make this a Yes Weekend, shall we?*

It was game on.

Five minutes later, the phone rings. It's my daughter.

"So, Mom," she says. "The girls and I were thinking. Why don't you come into the city and meet us? We could rent a hotel room and hang with my friends for the night. It would be a girls' weekend."

I smile on the other end. How wise was this wonderful universe? "OK!" I reply. Silence. "Hello? Sabrina? You there?"

"Mom? Did you just say yes?"

"I sure did!"

Minutes later I am off on my adventure. I go online and find a nice hotel. I book a room and pack a bag. Within an hour, I'm heading to Manhattan on my *Yes Adventure*. By the time I arrive and meet the girls, a storm has rolled in. Even though this makes the usual Manhattan traffic a bit more challenging, we have an amazing night together. The next morning, we meet over a delicious brunch. And because it's a *Yes Weekend*, I enjoy every bite of the pancake burrito on my plate.

By the time we return home, there is a glow on my face. Not only have I made new memories with my daughter, I have just been reminded that my *Yes Days* are good for the soul.

That's when I asked the question: *Why do we say no?*

Think about it. When was the last time you received an invitation and immediately replied by saying no? Really think about this. Did you decline because that wasn't where you wanted to spend your heartbeats? In that case, best decision ever, and congratulations on having clear boundaries. But if you said no because of fear, maybe it's time to open that toolbox of yours and get to work. Starting this moment, the next time you say no to something, pay attention to the why.

Sometimes I call my *Yes Days* my *Tracey Days*. I have my amazing husband to thank for that; he suggested I give these days a name to make the distinction between regular Stacey and Stacey without all the rules. He even came up with the name *stegan* to describe my version of going vegan, which I do every now and then. ("Oh, by the way, I'm vegan this month!") That's when I'll faithfully allow only vegetables on my plate, along with a small piece of chicken. As for Ed and how he came to be in my life, that's a word-centered story I love to tell.

FROM WORDS TO LIFE

I mentioned that it was while I was still in my first marriage (before my cancer diagnosis), I took the first real steps toward healing my broken spirit. I began reading anything I could find, becoming particularly intrigued with the subject of manifesting. The thought of using words to create one's life sounded so deliciously simple. Could this really be possible?

Soon, I was nose-deep in a workbook that helped get you in the habit of writing down your intentions. Not a day went by when I didn't open those pages with genuine intrigue and curiosity. I wanted to design a life filled with joy and contentment. Looking back, I was running into the arms of change.

As the months went by, I continued the healing process. I literally started looking at things differently: the trees, the flowers, the sky. I wanted to experience everything with fresh eyes. I wanted memories. I even had a motto:

> *No regrets. Stacey. Drink every drop of juice out of that box,*
> *and be mindful of where you spend your heartbeats.*

Once the cancer was behind me, I kept a journal to document all my new beliefs. On the left side, I would write down all that I was currently grateful for: health and waking up to another beautiful day were always at the top of my list. On the right side, I would write what I wanted to have in my life, but in the present tense. Always in my heart were my wishes for continued good health for me, my daughter, and my family and friends.

Then I started dabbling in the relationship world. The two words I kept writing repeatedly were *kind* and *healthy*. I would write, *I am in a relationship with a man who is kind and healthy. Our relationship is based on unconditional love and healthy interactions.* Every single day I would write out my thoughts. I wrote in such convincing language that when my soon-to-be ex happened to find this, he was convinced that I was writing about a new love interest. (What a fun conversation that was!) But I kept writing and writing—imagining, believing, and growing. *Butterfly, butterfly, fly, fly away!* And I did fly away from the marriage that was not meant for me.

I was now single and ready to experience the world in small steps. I wanted to see more of it. I had never been to Europe. My mom and I had been dreaming about going to Paris. We'd make it a girls' trip and include my sister and daughter. *Why wait? If not now, when?*

I remember hesitating briefly as I glanced at my new financial situation. It was still in postdivorce recovery. The old Stacey would have wagged a finger and told me to wait. This time, however, I decided that I would let faith do the talking. And it was telling me that money would come. I decided to listen. Before I knew it, we had the entire adventure booked and ready.

Everything was perfect. Even the missteps brought us joy—like the time we took the Eurostar train from Paris to London and hailed a cab to our hotel. My mom, forgetting that we were now in a country where drivers drove on the opposite side of the road, ended up accidentally opening the taxi driver's door and almost climbing onto his lap. We couldn't stop howling. I remembered thinking that I would spend every last penny I had on experiences and memories. I would live in the now.

By this time, I was living in my rented town house and diving deeper into my healing. I loved having the space just for my daughter and me; life seemed filled with possibilities. That two-bedroom home became our happy place and safe haven. I decorated it the way I wanted. The energy was peaceful. There was no yelling, no fighting, no fear, no eggshells to walk on—just beautiful wood floors, perfect for all the dancing we did when listening to music for hours.

I remember promising myself that, once I received the clear PET scan results, I would stop at nothing to live my best life. It would be by design, not default. That's when I really began watching where I spent my heartbeats. It was through this process that I realized just how many friends I had in my life who drained my energy.

- *Had they always been like that?*

- *How did I not notice?*

- *Was I once like that, too?*

Some were just demanding. Others were extremely negative, constantly calling to tell me about all the doom and gloom in the world. And there were a few—you know the ones; they call you up to have a "conversation," but what they really want is an audience for their monologue.

You set the phone down to put the laundry in the dryer, fix a snack, then pick the phone back up a few minutes later and they're still talking. And when you do manage to say something, your radar senses that they're not really listening to you. Their mind is already formulating their next answer. (On a side note, if you find yourself doing this, being more focused on squeezing something specific into the conversation instead of going with the flow, you may just want to check yourself. That's your ego grabbing the reins.)

Over time, I noticed that I began to have a little less patience for people who did not practice gratitude, or who felt entitled. I was all for helping others, and I did so any chance I could. But when people hold on to their drama like a badge of honor, sometimes it's healthier to let them go and find their own way in their own time. Some may even choose to stay on a sinking ship, and that's OK. Just know that you are free to take that lifeboat. Do not underestimate the joy of a low-maintenance friend. Yes, I said it—low maintenance.

The healthier I became, the better I was at smelling negativity, even from a mile away. I had just been given a second chance at life. I knew that life was too short to focus on what was wrong. As I started drifting away from toxic friends, the path before me began to clear, making way for new ones.

TAPPING INTO THE ENERGY OF WORDS

Have you ever noticed that people tend to reappear in your life just as you need them? Have you ever wondered why this happens? I believe this is our energy clearing the path for us because we've shifted our mindset. In my case, I was now focusing on the good I had in my life.

It was at this stage that I began rekindling old relationships with some amazing women. Some were also going through divorces. Meanwhile, I also became really close with my college friends and sorority sisters. Before I knew it, I found myself surrounded by a network of support.

Then, one day, I woke up. It was a Sunday. After getting my cup of coffee, I sat and thought, *Yeah. It would be nice to meet someone for coffee.*

After acknowledging my intention, I had to admit that I wasn't quite ready. I still wanted to explore the world and spend more time with myself. So, when a friend invited me to go to Italy with her, I jumped at the chance. The divorce now final, I was rebuilding financially, but trusted that it would all work out. I kept telling myself that money is like energy. It comes and goes. Have faith that it will all be OK. Not only did I go on the trip, I fell so crazy in love with Italy and its people that I told my girlfriend I wanted to be Italian. She laughed.

"You can't just wake up one day and be Italian, Stacey!"

It was on that trip that I decided, OK, I think I'm ready to meet someone for coffee. When I got back home, I decided to set up an account on one of the popular dating sites with a good track record. And I did go on a few dates, which led nowhere.

Then, late one Sunday night, when I was done with all the things I usually did on a Sunday—laundry, check; food shopping, check; dinner cooked, check; homework with Sabrina, check; work prep, check—I decided to open the app. *Maybe just one more time,* I said to myself.

And there he was. Right in the center of my page was this handsome man in a button-down shirt with the sleeves rolled up. He was hunched over in a bodybuilder pose—an adorable pretend growl on his face—his arms crossed in front of him. I looked closer. Tattooed on his arms were the words *Embrace* and *Change.*

Then I looked at his eyes. They were the kindest I had ever seen.

• • •

With each heartbeat you use to speak, whether to others or yourself, choose wisely. Go beyond just avoiding negative words. As much as possible—because each situation dictates what is practical and necessary—find a happy spin and put it out there. By making your default responses favorable ones, over time you will learn to develop a positive attitude. Once this becomes your natural "starting position," you will attract into your life more of what you truly want.

CHAPTER 7: KEY REMINDERS

- Whether we realize it or not, the quality of our lives–if not the very creation of it–lies in the power of our tongue.

- With every word, we create our reality.

- The trick is to use words and thoughts that support you. Fake it if you have to. Tell yourself that you can get to the other side of whatever challenging situation you're in. See it. Feel it. Then go for it.

- Deep down, most of us are hungry for words of encouragement. Even if we are considered experts at what we do, we still react with genuine appreciation when someone takes the time to support us.

- The healthier you become, the better you will be at sensing negativity in someone.

8

THE MAGIC
OF MANIFESTING

Have you ever met someone who narrowly escaped death? If not from a health scare, then a car accident or heinous crime gone awry? For some, the moment seemed to slow down while their peripheral vision closed in, heightening their sense of awareness. For the first time, their focus was the sharpest it had ever been. All they could see was the light at the end of that tunnel. And that moment—that reminder of life's fragility and wonder—stayed with them forever.

It was the same with me.

Once my brush with death was in my rearview mirror, I sent packing along with it my traumatized past. In its place came a sense of focus and presence that I had not had before. With this fresh perspective, I channeled my energy and heartbeats into manifesting all that I wanted for the rest of my life.

REAPING MY MANIFESTATION REWARD

There on my dating app page was the face of a handsome man with eyes that beamed with true kindness.

For a few moments, I stared at my screen, taking note of the fact that I was smiling on the outside *and* the inside. It was as if the universe had copied and pasted entire paragraphs from my journal of intentions and was now saying, "See? We were listening to you. Wish granted."

After studying Ed's picture, I read his profile because, yes, words matter. I had already been on a couple of dates, only to discover that what my dates had written did not quite match their reality. *You say you love to travel but have never actually been anywhere? You say family is important to you, but yet you've not spoken to your mom in how many months? Hmm. There goes that red flag.*

I liked how this Ed looked. So far, so good. But if there was even a hint of cruelty, cynicism, or anger in the words he chose, I would take a pass. There was none. Instead, I sensed only an inner peace and happiness. Even our taglines were matched. Mine said, *Make Today Count.* His said, *Get Busy Living.*

Coincidence? No way.

He had several other pictures around his brand, which I immediately checked out. A few with his dad were captioned: *A couple of generations of awesome.* I chuckled. *Humble, with a healthy sense of humor.* Another one of him in silly poses at the Grounds for Sculpture in Hamilton, New Jersey. *He's playful.* And another one in a business suit. *He gets the corporate world. I like that.* Encouraged by what I saw, I then read his description.

Pay attention to what people write and the words they use to describe themselves. You can learn a lot. Do they seem:

- Judgmental, negative, self-deprecating, cynical

or

- Hopeful, wide-eyed, humorous, energetic

If I didn't know better, I'd have sworn that Ed's near-perfect profile was too good to be true. Also recently divorced, this father of three spoke about self-awareness, about being raised by a single mom who had struggled financially, and about his respect for strong women. Our backgrounds could not have been more aligned.

Leaning forward in my chair, I took a closer look. Honestly, it was as if the universe was saying, "Let's just write this for you, Stacey."

I decided that I was going to reach out. Seconds later, fear started creeping in as I held my hands over the keyboard. But because I was practicing self-awareness—and you know that's the magic—I caught it. *Oh hello, fear! Well, well. Haven't seen you in a while. Let me show you the door. I'm too busy tonight to deal with you.* I continued to talk to myself, which is something I am constantly doing. *OK, Stacey, you have nothing to lose. Don't process, don't negotiate, just go for it, Miss Nike.* With fingers now in position, I took action.

"Hi there," I began. "I really like your profile. I would love to hear more about you."

And then I pressed "Send."

By this time, I had the whole profile-sifting process down pat with my family and friends. *What do we think of this guy?* (And don't pretend that's not what happens, because that's the dance!) But before anyone could get back to me with their opinions, Ed responded. And if you're assuming that he kinda liked my profile as well, I guess you'd be correct. There is, however, an important cautionary tale behind this that I'll share with you later on in this chapter.

For now, I could tell through the messages we were exchanging that he was indeed kind and had a healthy sense of humor and sharp wit. It was as if he had never had a disappointing day in his life, even though he had clearly had his own hurdles along the way. I also found out that he was dedicated to being a good dad to his son and two daughters. I knew this from the boundaries he was quick to show me.

When he found out where I lived, he almost ended it there, suggesting that meeting me was probably not a good idea after all. The last thing he wanted, he said, was the drama that could potentially develop if our kids were in the same school district.

I smiled.

This was no red flag. In fact, it was solid green. (Cue thunderbolt of joy.) He cared about protecting his children and had a strong sense of self-respect. This told me everything I needed to know.

Do you see the lesson here?

Remember: You will always win by showing someone your boundaries. Show the wrong people, and they'll disappear from your life. Show the right people, and they'll stay forever. The best part is the reputation you gradually build with yourself. Nothing makes you stand taller.

After assuring him that we were not in the same district, we took it to the next level—a big deal in the online world. That's right. We spoke in real time (drumroll) on the phone. I remember immediately thinking that I really liked the tone of his voice. For those of you who've ever dated online, you know how important this is. We compared our full schedules, trying to find a time when we could meet. But between personal and business travel, our first meetup kept being pushed down the calendar. Was this ever going to happen?

Then came a lucky break. We were able to make a date for a Thursday night almost three weeks after first communicating. As our date approached, we both became a little giddy. Finally, the big day arrived. But that morning, I woke up with a terrible sore throat. Later that day, I ran to the doctor to have it checked.

"It's strep throat, Stacey, and here is your prescription."

It's what?

I had never had strep before. *OK, universe. What gives?* For reasons I'll never know, I was not meant to meet Ed that night. Disappointed but determined to remain positive, I engaged in some calming self-talk, reminding myself to go with the flow. There is a reason for everything, even if we don't understand it. *Trust the process, Stacey. Don't force a circle into a square.*

I decided that this was a test. If Ed lost interest as a result of the delay, then he probably wasn't the guy for me. No better time to find out than now. I took a deep breath and called him with the news. But my fears immediately vanished with his reply. Not only was he understanding, he received the news with good humor, and we quickly rescheduled for the following Friday night.

At this point, he went dark. For those not familiar with online dating, this means that he pulled his profile down. I would later find out that, even before we met, he had decided to try online dating for a limited time. His next date, which happened to be with me, would be his last, regardless of the outcome. As it turned out, we had each been online dating for exactly three months.

Really? (Pause as the pieces effortlessly fall into place.)

This time, we were to meet at 6:00 p.m. at a restaurant in Randolph, New Jersey, where he was living at the time. When I woke up that Friday morning, the first thing I did was clear my throat. No strep stress in sight. *Thank you in advance, universe. This date is going to happen.*

That day at the office, I worked while watching the clock, eager for the moment when I could go home to get ready. I was sixteen all over again but with bills to pay and clothes with care labels that read *dry-clean only*. I still remember what I wore for our date after trying on no less than five outfits: white pants with a sleeveless black and white hibiscus shirt (as that's my favorite flower), and dangerously high platform sandals. He is six-foot-two, while I am five-four, so no judgment, please.

The clock in my car said it was 5:57 p.m. when I pulled into the parking lot. The engine now off, I took a final glance in the mirror and then reached for my phone.

Hi, I'm here, I wrote.

Hi, he replied. *I'm the handsome guy in the lobby.*

I giggled. *How cute.* His playful, confident reply was consistent with his profile. In that moment, he appeared even more attractive to me. Thankfully, when I walked into the lobby, there was only one man there. Potentially awkward situation thwarted. I approached him.

"Are you the handsome guy in the lobby?" I asked as if on a dangerous espionage mission.

We both laughed. As we were being led to our table, I noticed that he was wearing a wrinkled T-shirt and ripped jeans. *Hmm,* I thought to myself. *Odd for a Friday night.* But not wanting to judge, I let it go. It really didn't matter anyway. In that moment, I knew that this was going to be a positive interaction. The energy between us was already flowing. Nothing felt forced.

You've experienced this before, I'm sure. We can feel another person's energy, whether good or bad. It's as if our vibrations are having their own conversation but without words. We just have to eavesdrop and trust our guts. Mine was saying that all was well. *You are aligned, Stacey. Be yourself.*

For the next three hours, we talked nonstop about everything, including things that revealed what we were really like when no one was looking. For instance, when Ed mentioned that his Saturday plans included binge-watching a show with his dad, his stock value shot up even more in my eyes. This man was checking off almost every box on my list. I also asked him about the *Embrace Change* tattoos in his profile photo, which were now missing from his forearms. He explained that they had been temporary. They were part of a work assignment, the challenge being to find an expression that reflected your overall approach to your working life, but that could also be applicable to your personal life. I remember wishing the evening would never end. Eventually, though, it did. When the bill came, I automatically reached for my purse so we could split it, but he wouldn't have it. I smiled and graciously accepted his kindness. After he took care of the bill and thanked our waiter, Ed wrapped up our date by sharing with me one of his pet peeves: being late. That's when I found out the reason behind his casual attire.

Earlier that afternoon, he had stopped in at his office to deliver a package but then got stuck there unexpectedly. Realizing that he was running out of time, he had to make a decision: Go home to change as originally planned and be late, or show up on time for our date. Box checked. He decided that he wasn't going to be late, and that this would be an opportunity to test *me*. If I made his attire an issue, then I was not meant for him.

Our second date came soon afterward. This time, to make up for the torn jeans and wrinkled shirt, he booked a reservation at a swanky restaurant, and he wore a suit. He got double check marks for that. Once again, time stood outside the door as we laughed the entire evening. I kept thanking the universe for hearing me. I had never met anyone so kind.

For our third date, I asked him out to see the movie *Guardians of the Galaxy*. At this point, I was more than comfortable with him and also did not believe that a woman had to wait for the man to ask her out. Today, I still don't remember much about the movie. What I do remember, however, was feeling like a high school girl with a big crush on the school's popular, and very handsome, quarterback. Then, after the movie, he asked if I'd go steady with him.

"Steady?" I burst into a smile while he chuckled.

"Do people even call it that these days?" he asked. This time, we both laughed.

"Yes," I said. "Yes, I will go steady with you."

With that, together we embraced change and entered the next phase of our journey.

MANIFESTING OUR NEW LIFE

Ed and I were now dating exclusively. Even today, I still giggle when I say that.

Much to my delight, I discovered that, other than being an amazing guy, he had the same mindset as I had when it came to manifesting. When we didn't have our kids for the weekend, we would spend much of our time visualizing our future together through a game we called *Can You Imagine?*

When we went to Barbados on a holiday weekend, for instance, we sat by the pool holding hands and said, "Can you imagine a pool like this in our backyard?" When we went to a cozy bed-and-breakfast in Maine, we fell in love with the bench in the shower and the fireplace in the bedroom. So, we imagined both in our future house.

The entire time we were dating and manifesting our life together, I felt my soul was in it, and that I was its partner. This, I think, is what made the difference. It was the feeling of knowing in my soul that our wishes had already been granted. It was the kind of peaceful feeling that told you everything was as it should be. In many ways, it was like the warm and safe sensation you get when you've come home.

We continued visualizing like this until it was time to talk about moving in together. Talk turned into action, and we began looking in earnest. Because we had four kids between us—three girls and a boy—having enough bathrooms was high on our priority list. But for a while, nothing seemed to fit. Then, one day, Ed made the decision to open our search circle. Within a week of widening our search, we found one house that seemed promising and arranged to see it. When we got there, we were in such shock, for a few seconds all we could do was stare.

Not only did the house have the exact number of bathrooms we wanted, it had the same shape of pool we had seen in Barbados, a seated bench in the shower, and a gas fireplace in the bedroom. And there was more. What I didn't know, until then, was that my then-future husband had also been playing the *Can You Imagine?* game privately. To the list, he had secretly added glass blocks in the shower (not common at the time) and a tree house in the backyard. The house came with both.

• • •

One evening, while I was writing this chapter, Ed and I stopped to marvel at what we had visualized into existence. It was a beautiful, warm summer night. We had just finished some light chores, and were throwing out the garbage together at the end of our long driveway with Bella jumping around at our feet. After walking back to the house, we sat out on the front porch—just taking it all in with gratitude as the sun began to set. A mere five years ago we had seen this only in our minds. Today, it's ours and we are still pinching ourselves. In fact, every time we pay the mortgage, we high-five each other and say, "Thirty more days!"

But there was more.

There were two other items on my wish list that had also come true. You may remember that, years before when I was in my first marriage, I had started a journal of intentions in which I described the kind man to whom I was married. What I did not mention was that I had also described, in detail, the engagement ring he would give me.

When Ed asked me to marry him, he insisted that I describe in detail the kind of ring I wanted. And so, I told him about the ring I had described in my journal. And the other wish? That came to pass the day I walked down the aisle and took my new husband's family name—his Italian family name.

Do you have dreams you've not allowed your soul to imagine for fear of disappointment?

Push fear aside and step into your dreams.

For just one week, visualize your life in as much detail as you can. You have nothing to lose but a life of joy. Make it a private game—just you, your soul, and the universe. But for it to work, you have to really *feel* it. We are infinitely more powerful than we can imagine. Open your heart. Don't let that shutter close on you.

PUTTING AUTHENTICITY FIRST

When I think back to how Ed and I met, my palms get a little sweaty, but not always out of excitement. Here's one detail I did not mention: It was not my original profile that he saw. It was my second—my authentic profile.

The truth was when setting up my account, I was afraid of taking off that mask and being completely vulnerable. To protect myself, I wrote a very vanilla, almost generic profile, uploaded one of the photos I had taken in Italy—even though the hat I was wearing covered much of my face—and pressed "Send." *It'll do,* I told myself.

Looking back, I know I was hiding. I wasn't fooling anyone, though. My prospective dates sensed my attempt to shield my true self. My energy suggested that I wasn't entirely comfortable. As a result, I got very little interest coming my way. A few waves and winks. A wink? What does that even mean? Eventually, I took another look at myself. If I didn't know me, what would I have learned from my profile? Not much, I had to admit. And yet I had promised to be true to myself so I could design the life that I wanted. What a fraud I was! How could I manifest my dreams when I was not being myself?

I promptly rewrote my profile and updated it. Had I not done this, I would not be here today sharing the story of how this loving and supportive man came into my life. I know this because Ed, as I learned afterward, would first look at the profiles—which he called the "main meal." Only if satisfied with what he read would he then look at the photos—or "the dessert," as he called it.

The fear of taking that mask off—being your authentic self—is not to be underestimated. This is why most people live behind a facade. Only when something happens in their life to shake them awake do they "get it."

The good news is that you can't really hide from yourself for long. Your mind, body, and soul always know when you're betraying your true self. It knows when you're not at peace. The messages come in so many ways. You just have to pay attention:

- What's that back and neck pain really about?

- What about the chronic insomnia?

- And those frequent headaches?

Once you step into your authentic self, the path before you clears. Serendipities, the chills, the energy—you can almost feel it coursing through your body. Every time I look at Ed, I am reminded of this.

What about you?

What if you were meeting yourself for the first time?

1. What would your first impression be like? Be honest. Would you use words like *happy, content, engaging, hopeful, enthusiastic, or curious*?

2. Would you leave your company feeling that you had just been in the presence of someone who loves themselves?

3. Would you think, "Now here's someone honoring their heartbeats."

Many of us grapple at some point or the other with embracing authenticity. We think that if we show our true selves we will be judged, possibly ridiculed, maybe even ostracized. We hide all the imperfect pieces because we think it is too painful to be vulnerable. We would rather spend our energy looking the other way. The truth is, we could spend our entire lives living like this and be OK. But what, then, would we be manifesting? A life that is not truly aligned with what we want? A life that works perfectly for someone else, but not for us?

I did this for the duration of my first marriage. I was always pretending to be someone I was not—the happy wife in a happy marriage with the white picket fence. But behind the facade, my soul was crying to break free. It took cancer to get me to a place that was so raw, I no longer could, or wanted, to hide.

I'm here to remind you that everyone struggles with something at some point. Everyone. That's what makes us human. In fact, not only can opening up be a catalyst for growth, it increases the chances of making real and lasting connections with others. Make a conscious effort to embrace your authentic self. It's the first step to manifesting the life you truly want.

If you need a little encouragement, let's take a quick look at those who don't seem to care as much about how they appear in the eyes of others.

WALKING THAT FINE LINE

I'm sure you've met people in your life who seem to be highly intuitive. Perhaps you're one. You seem to be able to understand people, even with little interaction. You may even be able to read a room with a fair degree of accuracy. And if this sounds like a cool super power to have, it is, particularly when you're in the business world. But there is a possible downside to having this kind of emotional connection.

More often than not, people like this tend to be highly adaptable—we could even say *malleable*. And while it's nice to be nice, they also run the risk of becoming people pleasers. That, of course, is not what we want. Remember those healthy boundaries we've worked so hard to build?

What, then, can we learn from those who do not possess this trait? I'm talking about people who don't seem to care much about how others perceive them. They speak their minds, dress as they wish, do what pleases them, and make no apologies for doing so. Have you ever met such a person? I find I can spot them like that (snaps fingers). In my opinion, they're fascinating to watch.

What can we learn from these amazing individuals?

It's true that in a few cases, they may not have the likeability factor that you do, but damn, they're not afraid! There's no fear because they don't know how to give a (bleep). While they may be kind and even generous, they're not trying to accommodate anyone's mood or agenda or expectations. You look at them and almost see this unshakable confidence. They know who they are and they like what they see.

It's the kind of self-acceptance that makes you say, "Waiter, I'd like to order two of what they're having, please!" And why not? These individuals sleep soundly at night because they're happy in their own skins. More often than not, they're usually quite successful at manifesting the lives they want, which oftentimes makes them among the most respected.

• • •

We each have just one chance at life. One.

Decide that you're going to use your precious heartbeats to design the life of your dreams. You can do it. There is no feeling more wonderful than mentally standing tall, throwing your arms open wide, and saying, "This is me, and this is what I want!" You have a rightful place in this world and a purpose that only you can fill. Believe in yourself. Invest in your vision and really see it happening.

Can you imagine?

CHAPTER 8: KEY REMINDERS

- Whether a health scare or some other traumatic event that's now in the past, use it to channel your energy and heartbeats into manifesting all that you want for the rest of your life.

- When visualizing something you want, first see it in your soul and then see yourself as your soul's partner in manifesting this dream.

- For just one week, visualize your dream life in as much detail as you can. You have nothing to lose but a life of joy. Make it a private game—just you, your soul, and the universe. But for it to work, you have to really *feel* it. We are infinitely more powerful than we can imagine. Open your heart.

- Embracing your authentic self is the first step to manifesting the life you truly want.

- Can you imagine?

IN THE END,
EACH NEW DAY IS
A NEW BEGINNING

As I write this closing chapter, summer has long made its exit from the Northeast.

The occasional early arctic blast aside, I'm a bit of a sucker for the fall vibe. With it comes that certain softening of the sun's light, the smell of cinnamon in the air, and the unmistakable wink from the holiday season reminding us that it is just around the bend. And because of where I live, I get to enjoy the miracle of nature that is the majestic changing of the leaves and experience the gradual dipping of those daily temperatures. But for me, this November brings more; it delivers a reminder of the past.

As a survivor of a life-threatening disease, I can tell you that the postcancer life is special in many ways. The most obvious is that you are forever filled with joy and gratitude for the second chance you've been given to honor your life with all your hopes and good intentions. With each day—yes, with each heartbeat—you open your eyes and get to walk through this world with a perspective few have.

There is, however, a bit of a *but*. Because you once faced a monster, the reality is that you are always on the lookout for its return. You are always managing your own version of PTSD. While the worry gets softer and lower in volume, it never really goes away. This makes for a somewhat awkward dance between staying positive and staying real.

In my case, it means seeing my oncologist every six to eight months so I can take a snapshot of how I'm looking. And that time has rolled around once more.

To prepare for my checkups, I do an aggressive cleanse about a month before my appointments and keep my family, bosses, and close friends in the loop. Support, after all, is paramount. For the entire time while waiting for the results, I pull out every tool I have and then some to keep the smile on my face. This includes writing in my journal where I tell myself that I am healthy today and am no longer at *dis-ease*. I stay in the present because it is the only thing that's real.

Tomorrow, as they say, is promised to no one. It is a truth I have long learned.

While I am able to remain in a state of relative calm, I know that fear is ready to pop up at any given moment. I kid you not when I say that I could literally burst into tears if I went to my pantry right now and discovered that I'm out of coffee.

• • •

Now for the backdrop story.

As I said in the introduction, when I first wrote the opening lines to this book in the spring of 2021, I had but one reason to share my experience: to encourage others to make their own lives even a little better—to become the most amazing expression of themselves they could be.

But then, at some point, along came the genesis of a second purpose. While at the time it was not clearly defined, there was, in fact, a sense in me that this book could also be part of a path to a life beyond the one I was currently enjoying in corporate America. Then, as the months went by, like a song that floats into your head in your quiet moments, the thought of being a life coach began to flicker in my mind now and then.

Stacey, what's this all about?

The truth is I had always reveled in the role of mentor. Second only to reaching my targets and making my bosses happy, there was just something about uplifting others that always managed to put a glow in my cheeks. It made my heart sing. In fact, I always secretly thought of it as the best job perk ever.

So, I started to self-talk about it. *Could you really do that, Stacey? Could this be the other reason you're writing the book? OK, this could be a possibility, but only after you've put in another twenty years. You love your life as it is way too much. You could never leave. You'd miss it. You know you would. Let's put this in the TBD file for now.*

For months I went about quietly having this private conversation.

It had never been my intention to change anything about my life where my career was concerned. I had fallen in love with the energy of corporate America since the first day I walked through its doors almost three decades earlier.

Not only did I grow up there, I considered myself a lifer. And it had been more than good to me. Look in my closet and you would know you were looking at someone who couldn't wait to wake up and get dressed each morning so she could tackle another day, even with the signature stress. Because, yes, my friends, with corporate America comes a healthy dose of that wild adrenaline rush. It can be quite the rollercoaster. But I had grown so used to it that it didn't occur to me that there was another way to live other than with my hair slightly on fire.

Still determined to remain where I was, I nevertheless began to listen to my gut—because you always have to listen closely. Then, as the summer approached, I did a little research on the side and scratched the itch further by signing up to train after-hours for my life coach certification. It was like my first day at my job all over again. I was in love and eager to keep exploring. For the time being, that was good enough for me.

However, once I began to see that this second path was taking on more definition, the questions began to come at me even faster. *What do you really want to do? What about carrying both careers at the same time? Do you think that could work? Would that even be allowed?* Honestly, at times I felt like a solo stage actor playing two parts: the wise guidance counselor and the confused, pimply-faced senior.

By the time fall arrived, I knew I was at the proverbial fork in the road. *Which way will you go, Stacey?* When the internal dialogue began to consume me, I reached for my favorite tool—my Stethoscope Gut Check—and put the question to the universe. There was no reason for me to obsess about the right answer; it would appear when it was meant to appear. In the meantime, my heartbeats were focused elsewhere. With my checkup tests just weeks away, I needed to channel my energy into remaining calm and positive.

• • •

I was going to soak up the 2021 holiday season as if it were my first. The pause in my life that was my series of checkup tests now behind me, I could once again breathe knowing that I was going to be just fine.

One mid-December day, out of the beautiful blue, my mind turned to a longtime colleague and friend with whom I had not spoken for quite some time. Like another favorite song I had not heard in ages, her name popped into my head. *Call Rose*, the whisper said. I ignored it at first, thinking it too random. After the third time, however, I heeded the nudge and called her. Catching up with ease as only old friends can, I eventually updated her on the decision before me, telling her that while I was excited about my options, I was still not sure which choice was right for me at this stage.

An hour-long conversation ensued. We went wide and deep. By the time the call ended, I had made my decision. In my mind's eye, I was now standing before the door I had been longing to open. For the first time in months, I felt lighter; the internal conversation I had been having was suddenly over. The chatter was gone. All I needed to do now was turn the knob and walk right in. I was one step away.

• • •

Only a day or two later, I was in my home office rummaging through my desk for something Ed needed. You might remember my mentioning in the introduction that while I am surface neat, those hidden spaces of mine—drawers in particular—are not to be trusted. You enter at your own risk.

Midway through my search, one of them jammed. It would neither open fully nor close no matter how I shook it or tried to jostle the items around. I decided to get back to it after going through the remaining drawers. Once I had finished, I returned to the stubborn drawer. But still, it refused to budge. *What could be stuck in there?* Frustrated, I got up to get a glass of water. When I returned a few minutes later, I sat in my chair and stared at the half-open compartment. *I'm going in.*

This time, after a little shuffling and rearranging, I was able to grab the item that was creating all the fuss; it was a book. Given my appetite for reading, that was not a surprise. But when I turned it over to see the cover, I gasped softly. It was one of my favorite Oprah Winfrey books, *The Path Made Clear: Discovering Your Life's Direction and Purpose.*

Sitting there alone, I ran my hand lightly over the cover. *Of course,* I thought, smiling to myself. *Of course, it would be this book.* If I needed a sign with which to finally seal my decision, I had just received it. I would step aside from corporate America and prepare for a new life.

Had you told me a year ago that I'd be making a lane change after almost thirty years of an exciting career in corporate America, I would have laughed and shaken my head with a polite, "No, I really don't think so."

But when I look behind me, I can't help but see the stepping-stones that got me to this point. They're so clear now, that when I turn to look ahead of me, I can already see the landscape of my future. I see the workshops I want to coach or lead. I see the amazing people I'll be meeting—individuals who need help to overcome obstacles in their private and professional lives. And I can even feel the energy surge within me as I use my heartbeats to build something new and wonderful.

Once again, I am choosing a leap of faith because I know I am meant to be here. Everything happens for a reason. And I am exactly where I need to be.

I implore you now to do the same.

Choose faith over fear each and every time. Decide today that you're going to take control of your life. No other heart beats the way yours does. And there is a reason for that. There's only one you.

Take those steps you've been longing to explore and feel the excitement of being expansive in your mind and heart. Keep going. One day, when you stop to look behind you, you'll be amazed at the miracle you've created for yourself one beautiful heartbeat at a time.

TOOLBOX SUMMARY AND EXERCISES

This is a compilation of the tools mentioned in the book, plus others that I have found to be helpful in my journey. Have fun by adding your own tweaks so they can be even more effective for you.

BEST-FOR TEST

Strangers and acquaintances aside, have you ever asked yourself how those in your inner circle affect you? After all, you spend a good deal of your heartbeats on them. Whenever you're unsure of how someone is impacting your life, take a quick test. Even though you were once heavily invested in their lives, it may be that things have changed. You begin to wonder if they are still the best company for you. Ask yourself these questions:

1. Do you still feel they bring out the best in who you are, or do you find yourself now feeling a bit agitated?

2. Do they seem interested in what you bring to a conversation, or do you sense that they're more interested in lining up their next response?

3. Do you find yourself wondering how soon you can make an exit, or does time seem to fly by when you're with them?

4. Do you feel like yourself when you're in their company, or do you notice that you hold back on certain aspects of your personality?

5. Do you feel energized or generally uninspired about the things you talk about?

6. Do you feel better about yourself when you leave them, or do you feel as if you could have spent your time more wisely?

BREATH TRANSFUSION

Nothing restores calm and focus like deliberate breathing. In this exercise, imagine giving yourself a breath transfusion as you breathe in strength and exhale fear:

1. Close your eyes.

2. Imagine that the air you're about to take into your body is infused with strength. If it helps, picture it as a certain color.

3. Take a deep breath while counting to four.

4. Imagine the air you have just inhaled going through your body and pushing out the fear trapped inside you.

5. Now, exhale all the fear while counting to four. As you did with the strength you inhaled, give the fear a color as you picture it rushing out of your body.

6. Repeat several times until you feel the calm returning.

CAN YOU IMAGINE?

Visualization is nothing new, of course. This comes second nature to us as children. As we grow older, however, we tend to let go of that side of us that imagines in detail and without restraint. The trick here is to name the process that makes visualization real for you. Once you tell yourself that you're playing your _____ (insert name) game, you automatically give yourself permission to dive deep, just as I did when healing from cancer, and as Ed and I did when searching for our home. Remember to relax, and really let yourself get into as much detail as you want. The only rule is that limitations are not allowed.

CHECKING THE SCALES

This is another version of the Stethoscope Gut Check. When I have an important (usually life-changing) decision to make, I check the scales to see how I'm feeling. This is the test I used most when trying to decide whether to remain in an unhealthy marriage.

1. Picture both your decisions on each scale. For the abovementioned scenario, it was *stay* (left scale) and *leave* (right scale).

2. Without thinking, because you want to be as honest as possible, allow yourself to feel which is heavier.

3. Do this regularly and see if there's a pattern. On a side note, you will find yourself struggling the most when the scales seem to be evenly balanced. This is because you will find yourself questioning everything. Don't worry. You won't stay in this place forever. At some point, something will tip the scales permanently.

4. When the scales finally stop moving back and forth, you have arrived at your true decision.

DETACHMENT

When I find myself dealing with anxiety or worry, I find it helpful to mentally step back and become the observer. While it may not result immediately in a solution, it often brings me some perspective that might have been lost and gives me a moment to catch my breath. Here are two techniques that can be done anywhere, even when in public.

OUTER SPACE

1. Sit quietly, and imagine that you're in a spaceship waiting to be launched into outer space. The doors are closed, and no one is able to enter that capsule with you.

2. The engines ignite. Tell yourself that, for a few minutes, you're going to leave your source of angst behind.

3. You have liftoff. As you climb higher and higher, Earth becomes smaller and smaller. At the same time, so does the problem you're grappling with.

4. You're now in outer space. You're literally floating and all is quiet. Earth is now so small you could almost hold it in your hands. Feel your anxiety disappear for even a few moments.

TV SHOW

1. Imagine that you're sitting on your couch and have just turned on the television.

2. The show that comes up is about you.

3. Watch the events unfold as if watching a documentary. You might just see a new perspective that helps you find a solution.

HEARTBEAT STOCKTAKING

Just as a business takes inventory, we should also take note of where we spend our heartbeats. Your reasons could fall into any category—from how much time you spend exercising, doing housework, or socializing to how much time you spend working. Here are just a few examples I gathered from friends and acquaintances:

- Brianna, who likes a tidy house and home-cooked meals, always suspected that she was spending too many hours cleaning, cooking, and doing laundry. While she was proud of the clean and orderly nest she had created, she felt that her home-based business was suffering. She decided to track her time for two weeks. Much to her shock, she found that she was averaging fourteen hours each week alone on house chores—practically an entire day each week.

- Shannon, a self-declared minor hot mess, had the opposite challenge. Not the most organized person, she was almost always searching through pockets of clutter for her personal and other items. When it finally reached the point where she felt her quality of life was being affected, she decided to track the amount of time she spent putting out those small self-imposed fires. "It was an eye-opener," she said. "I was spending almost an hour a day looking for things I needed—from car keys to sunglasses to bills. Not only did the endless searching often cause me to be constantly chasing deadlines, I felt that I was living with a chronic low-grade stress I had come to accept as normal. That was when I knew things had to change."

- As her third decade of her corporate life approached, Terry began to feel the wear and tear of her hectic workdays. Still keeping up with the pace, she secretly wondered whether she needed to reassess her working life. "I began to notice that we would have back-to-back meetings, with literally no time scheduled in between for even a quick bathroom break," she said. "It was a small thing, of course, but it made me sit up and wonder where I wanted to be five years down the line."

LOOKING INTO THE KALEIDOSCOPE

Whenever I'm having a difficult time with something or am feeling stressed, I use this tool to restore a sense of calm. For me, this is another version of reminding myself that this too shall pass. I remind myself that if I give it time (a day, or two, or more) I might see it differently.

1. Imagine that you're looking into a kaleidoscope.

2. In it, you see the situation that's causing you some stress.

3. Picture yourself turning the barrel ever so slightly so that the image changes.

4. Remind yourself that this has happened to you before, because life, like a kaleidoscope, is always changing.

5. Keep turning until the situation no longer seems as dire.

6. Lock into that more upbeat image and feeling.

7. Allow it to expand.

MEET AND GREET

Use this tool when encountering an unpleasant challenge for the first time.

1. Tell yourself that you've just encountered something interesting, and that you're about to learn a valuable skill or lesson. Remind yourself that even if you go through some unpleasant moments, you will emerge wiser than before.

2. Identify the lesson(s) being sent your way. This will require you to remain calm and clear-eyed so you can sift through what may initially appear as random debris.

3. Let the lessons flow through you without your biases filtering them.

RETURNING TO THE PLAYGROUND

When we find ourselves in the presence of an aggressive person who threatens to raise our anxiety thermostat, we sometimes find ourselves reacting when we should be responding. The next time you find yourself in this situation, try this simple perception adjustment. For this example, imagine that you're in a meeting led by someone who is being unusually relentless.

1. As you sit at the table, step back in your mind and picture this person as a young child at the neighborhood playground. They're in their little shorts and T-shirt. Maybe they've just had some ice cream, and there are chocolate stains all around their mouth.

2. Watch them kicking their little legs high and squealing while on the swings. See them rolling in the sand. Hear them laughing with joy as they sail down the slide. Once upon a time, they, too, were just a kid.

3. Notice a sense of compassion taking over. Now that you've taken the edge off your anxiety, you should find that you're able to respond in a controlled manner rather than reacting without thinking.

REWINDING AND RECALIBRATING

Use this tool to evict those deep-seated fears that have come to stay. For this example, imagine the fear of growing old, alone, and lonely:

1. Lean into your fear as if watching a movie. See yourself alone in your house day after day. Feel the isolation.

2. Hit "Pause" on this thought and freeze this image. Take a good look at "the screen." Tell yourself that it doesn't have to be this way. Tell yourself that this will not be your life's standard.

3. What's the opposite of your biggest fear? Picture it in your mind.

4. Zoom in, and see what that would be like. This time, you're constantly surrounded by family and friends. You're always going out to social events and must often decline invitations. The phone is always ringing. You're a fixture at many charity events. Are you there?

5. Hit "Rewind," and keep replaying the new thoughts until you are immersed in this new scenario.

6. Recalibrate your thoughts around this image. From now on, this is your standard. Whether with affirmations, self-talk, or visualization, you will diffuse all thoughts of that old fear. It no longer exists.

SELF-CARE

Self-care is not selfish. Even though we all know this, I still feel we can't hear it enough. (You know how quick we are to feel guilty when we're not being productive.) If you don't have a list, build one now to reinforce the fact that you deserve it. This is what mine looks like:

1. *Support groups.* Whether it's official organizations (e.g., for cancer survivors) or the friends you can call at 3:00 a.m., surround yourself with people you can turn to for help when you need that extra shoulder.

2. *Exercise.* With every step you take, you are showering your body with love and giving your heart more life. When I exercise and feel my heart beating, I tell myself that I am giving it a hug.

3. *Music and videos.* From music to inspirational videos, I have my go-to playlists and YouTube videos that give me that lift when I need it. Are there certain songs that always make you want to sing? Are there special motivational speakers that bring you clarity? Take the time to compile a list. Take them with you while you're exercising or taking a walk.

4. *Grooming.* In addition to keeping my nails clean and neat, I like to wear nail polish colors that make me smile. In fact, I like this aspect of my self-care so much, I sometimes thank other ladies for brightening my day with their colorful choices.

5. *Hot beverage treats.* Sometimes when I want to feel comforted, I prepare myself a hot beverage as if it were a ritual. I'll select a favorite mug, make my brew, and go to a special place in my house that makes me happy. Depending on how I'm feeling, this may be where the sun is shining, where a blanket is waiting, or where I can put my feet up. And then I'll sip slowly, taking note of each mouthful as it goes down. This treat, for however long it lasts, is my way of soothing myself.

6. *Focusing on others.* As odd as it may sound, helping others has the magical effect of temporarily taking the focus off of you. And if that person benefits from your kindness, the happiness you feel can only help ease your own pain.

7. *Using reminders.* From calendars on my desk, to personal notes on the mirror, to T-shirts that say it for me, I surround myself with words of encouragement in any way I can. Because on the days when I'm not feeling it from within, I can't go too far without being reminded how powerful I am and how much I've overcome.

SELF-TALK

As I mentioned, I talk to myself a lot, particularly when trying to keep fear at bay. And if I'm alone, I'll say the words out loud and even look into a mirror if I can, as if talking to a friend. This forces you to be careful about the words you choose. Here are a few examples:

- "Stacey, today is the only thing you need to worry about. In fact, this moment is the only thing you need to focus on right now because tomorrow is promised to no one."

- If I'm in a meeting and feeling nervous, I tell myself that every single person sitting at that table is going through something. "Not only is no one here better than you are, Stacey, beneath that calm exterior they may also be just as nervous."

- If something is causing me stress, I say, "Stacey, I think you've been through challenges that are *much* scarier. You've got this."

- I use a HAPPY reminder list. Say to yourself, "_____, *I want you to remember:*"

  (Just)   How far you've come.
  (The)   Amazing things you've done.
  (How)   Powerful you really are.
  (The)   People who love you.
  (That)   You are *never* alone.

SHOWDOWN WITH FEAR

To fear is to be human. The goal is to not let it paralyze you.

1. Picture your worst possible fear standing right in front of you.

2. Stare it down. Look at its shape and angles.

3. Say, "OK, I see you. I get what you're all about. And?" At this point, a sense of acceptance and calm should begin to seep in.

4. Now imagine looking over its shoulder. What do you see next? You might be surprised to find that you're looking at a possible solution.

STETHOSCOPE GUT CHECK

Do you have an important decision to make? As we all know, our gut instincts are almost always right. Train yourself to listen carefully:

1. Imagine yourself going with one decision. See yourself going with that scenario. Picture the smallest details: the people, the location, the change of pace, the weather, the sounds, the smells, maybe even a change of language or culture— immerse yourself in it.

2. Take a deep breath and listen to what your gut is telling you. Notice your feelings for what they are without judging or trying to understand them.

3. Imagine yourself going with the other decision, and dive into it as deeply as you did above.

4. Take another deep breath, and listen to what your gut has to say about that scenario.

5. Take note of which option makes your body feel instantly calmer. Which situation makes you breathe more easily? Which causes your shoulders to relax? Which gives you angst? Which makes your heart smile? Which makes you literally smile?

6. Ask the universe for guidance and direction by giving you a clear sign.

7. Let it go and wait.

TACTFUL DIRECTNESS

It is never easy to confront someone when feelings have been hurt or boundaries have been crossed. For the sake of maintaining a healthy self-esteem, however, it is necessary. I have found this approach to be useful whether in business or personal relationships.

1. Ask the person if they have a moment. This shows that you respect their time and do not wish to bulldoze them. If you don't do this and immediately bring up the issue, they will either shut down or become defensive.

2. Start with something positive. It's important that you choose something you sincerely like or appreciate about what they did. If not, your tone will belie your words.

3. Put the issue on you. In other words, tell them that you're feeling a certain way about something they said or did. By suggesting that this is a possible misinterpretation on your part that may or may not be valid, the other person is less likely to go on the defensive.

4. Remain silent while you wait for the other person to speak. Do not ramble just to fill the awkward silence.

Here's a workplace example:
You walk into a meeting in which you're about to provide an update and see that in attendance is a colleague known for interrupting meetings, usually in an attempt to steer the conversation his way. For the sake of your self-esteem, it's important that you tackle this as soon as you can. You do this by: 1) addressing the issue as it happens, and 2) speaking to your peer privately afterward to reinforce your position..

Your approach may go something like this. During a meeting after he has just interrupted you, say, "Great point, Dave, and after my update we can pivot to your topic."

Then, after the meeting, say, "Hey, Dave, do you have a minute? There's something I'd love to talk to you about."

"Sure, Stacey. I'm free now."

"Great. Listen, I really appreciate your knowledge and contribution to our meetings. They've been helpful. And in the future, so that we don't miss anything, I'd prefer you wait until after I've finished my thoughts."

Remain silent and let Dave reply.

Here's an example of a more personal nature:

You confide in your friend, Samantha, that you've just had an argument with your brother. As this rarely happens, you're upset by it but remain confident that you'll sort it out. A few days later, you, Samantha, and another friend go out for a pre-Thanksgiving lunch. The discussion turns to the upcoming holiday season and family gatherings. At this point, Samantha begins looking at you knowingly while making comments about how awkward it can be around the dinner table when there's a family rift. You shift in your chair and successfully manage to change the conversation. At this point, you want to do two things:

1. Question the trust level of this friendship. Perhaps Samantha is no longer the friend you thought she was.

2. Be true to yourself. The fact of the matter is Samantha crossed a line, whether intentionally or not. Either way, for your sense of self-respect, you should address it.

Your approach may go like this after the meal is over.

"Hey, Samantha, do you have a minute? There's something I want to talk to you about."

"Sure, Stacey, how about now?"

"I really enjoy our ladies' lunches. They're a good stress buster. I noticed that during our conversation, however, you were hinting at the rift between my brother and me. I have to tell you I was surprised since I had told you about it in confidence."

Remain silent, and let Samantha explain.

• • •

BEFORE YOU GO

In the preceding chapters, I touched on several related subjects that I did not delve into. This was deliberate on my part. While I felt *them to be important, I did not want to distract the reader from the book's core message. That said, I feel compelled to share some of these real-life experiences before you go. Take from them whatever help or wisdom you can glean.*

BEING THE CEO OF YOUR BODY

While it was not my intention to make this book about my cancer journey, I would be remiss if I didn't say something about managing our physical health, listening closely to our bodies, and listening to our gut instincts.

In 2010, I was diagnosed with stage-zero breast cancer, had a double mastectomy shortly thereafter, and was sent home with a 95 percent survival rate. All of us—my doctors, family, and I—had every reason to believe that I would be fine; cancer was no longer an issue for me. But only two years later—*two short years*—I started to feel an odd pain under my right arm. *Hmm,* I thought. *That's weird.* But as I had always had intermittent pain after my surgery, I was quick to dismiss it. Or, I should say, I tried to.

The truth was, deep down, I knew this pain was different. I started feeling around my armpit and thought I detected a very teeny, tiny lump. But again, as sometimes our mind plays tricks on us, I told myself that it was my active imagination. *It couldn't be,* I thought. *We caught it at stage zero! Nah!*

Several days later, however, I decided to see my doctor anyway. After all, you can never be too safe. My doctor did not seem worried either, but ordered some blood work to check my markers. A few days later, I received the news that while they were only slightly elevated, I had nothing to worry about. That said, my doctor and I agreed that we would test again a few weeks later, which we did. Much to my relief, those test results showed no change.

In the days that followed, I continued about my life, all the while secretly feeling that something was off. Soon after, I flew to California for a leadership meeting. As I was getting ready, for some reason, I touched my neck in the area near my clavicle. That's when I felt it: a soft, squishy, almond-shaped lump. The blood drained from my face; I almost fainted. I don't know how I did it, but somehow, I pushed myself through my meetings with a plastic smile on my face. The only thing I could think of was getting home so I could see my doctor again.

Days later, I was in my doctor's office. I knew that this time I was not going to be told that it was nothing. We planned the biopsy, which was scheduled for a Saturday. That alone said a lot. Lying on the operating table, I distracted myself at the beginning of the procedure by thinking back to the news I had seen that morning, when I learned that a hurricane named Sandy was barreling its way toward us. *I'm sure it'll be fine.* Those were my last words to myself before I drifted off.

When I woke up, the doctors gave me the dreaded news: It was malignant. And there was more. They would have to run tests to find out what kind of cancer it was. The results would be back in ten to fourteen days.

I went home numb.

How would I make it through the next two weeks? That kind of wait—not knowing if you're going to make it or not—is something I wish on no one. Then, just two days later, on October 29, Hurricane Sandy hit the New Jersey area. We lost electricity for almost a week and were literally eating canned and boxed food.

I had never felt so alone in this world.

I was literally in a dark house, stuck in a deeply troubled marriage, and struggling to appear upbeat for my beautiful ten-year-old daughter whom I didn't want to burden with my journey, all while quietly picturing my sad, little biopsy tube sitting somewhere in a lab that no one could reach. All I wanted to know was whether I was going to live or die. That was the epitome of fear. For the entire time, I breathed, prayed, and told myself that no matter what, I would make it. And while I did make it through, I will always remember those two weeks as the darkest days of my life.

To reinforce my message, I'll share the story of my mom, whose brush with cancer I alluded to in Chapter 2. One day, she noticed something on her arm that didn't look right. She immediately went to see a dermatologist, who told her that it was nothing, that it was just from the sun. But even as my mom walked out of the doctor's office with this good news, she felt in her gut that something was wrong. Stopping at the receptionist's desk, she asked for an appointment with another dermatologist for a second opinion. When she was told that she couldn't have one since her doctor had given her a clean bill of health, my mom sat down. She was not leaving until she had that appointment. Finally, she was granted one with another doctor, who ordered the biopsy that confirmed that my mom, in fact, had stage-one melanoma.

I share these two stories with you as a reminder that we are the CEOs of our bodies. Doctors are the experts, and they are there to help and support us. But it is our responsibility—100 percent—to manage, advocate, and do what we must to ensure our health. Listen to your gut instincts. Continue to press. Never take no for an answer. Nobody knows your body like you do. No one.

STAYING FOR THE CHILDREN

I am a bit hesitant to weigh in on this topic, as everyone has their own view, and I respect that. Every journey, every situation, is different.

When I started my adult life as a child of divorced parents, I was adamant that, no matter what, I would stay in my marriage forever; if not for me, then for my child. I would work through whatever the issue was. It was one and done for me. I truly believed that and walked the talk for twenty years. That changed one day while I was home after a chemotherapy treatment.

I was sitting on the couch with my beautiful bald head, cuddled up with a blanket, and sipping a cup of tea. That day, my daughter witnessed an unhealthy interaction between her father and me. He had raised his voice at me again. This time, tired and weakened by chemotherapy and stress, I just couldn't take it anymore. I broke down crying in front of my daughter, something I had always tried not to do. And on a side note, even if children don't hear their parents' conversations or see their interactions, they know and sense exactly what's going on. Your template almost inevitably becomes part of the fabric of who they are and determines how they act in their own relationships.

But then, in that moment, the mama bear in me roared awake. Sound the alarms! The traffic light just turned green, and it's time to switch roads! When you realize you're impacting another person such as a child, the choice becomes clear. I knew I had to go.

Fast-forward to a beautiful day in May 2021. My daughter and I are driving home and have just gone past a beautiful local farm. I remember looking at all the fresh veggies in the front stand and thinking how pretty all the colors are. I tell myself that it's a nice reminder that I should eat more foods from the rainbow of colors. Then, mid-reverie, I hear my daughter's voice.

"Mom?" she says. "Thank you."

"For what?" I ask with a smile. "I haven't bought you anything. We're just driving home."

"No. I mean thank you for taking charge of your life. For showing me what's possible."

In that moment, tears filled my eyes. If I didn't know it before, I knew it then. Had I stayed in my first marriage, not only would my physical and mental health have been affected, but my precious daughter's emotional health would have been, too. That's when I knew, without a doubt, that I had made the right decision.

CHOOSING YOUR LIFE PARTNER

Everyone has their own set of hopes and expectations where their mate is concerned. Mine became very clear only after I had already married my high school sweetheart. When it comes to deciding on the person with whom to walk through this world, my simple advice is to first look for someone who is kind.

When you're with someone who honestly loves and understands you, they will naturally stay away from your insecurities. They will build you up. They won't push your buttons. They won't prey on your fears. They don't want to see you hurt or suffer if they can help it.

I suppose you could say, "Yes, but, Stacey, we can control our reactions." The short answer to that is, yes, but only to an extent. Ultimately, it's easier and more joyful to be with someone who simply doesn't go there—who doesn't put you in an unhappy position, forcing you to push back or put up your armor. That's no way to live.

My marriage to Ed is like a fluid dance. We are not perfect, but each step comes so easily and naturally that it hardly requires much effort. There is no ego involved, no posturing for power, no demands or pressure of any kind. It is a relationship based on unconditional kindness. Ed encourages me to go in any direction that makes me happy. He was right there cheering me on from the moment I whispered my first thoughts of writing this book. And he continued to do so until I had written the final page.

You deserve someone who loves you unconditionally. Tell yourself this every day, and you will recognize this person once they appear before you. I have felt nothing but joy and gratitude since the day I married Ed. If after leaving a toxic relationship you are blessed to find someone amazing to love, you never quite stop glancing over at that person with that pinch-me-before-I-wake-up feeling. And every now and then, life sends us little reminders of just how lucky we are.

• • •

Over the Fourth of July holiday of 2021, Ed and I took a little weekend getaway in Atlantic City to spend some time together. Although we like to play blackjack from time to time, we are not big into gambling. What we love, however, is the energy of the restaurants, outlets, and people. For us, Atlantic City is just one of those places we get to plug into and leave feeling recharged.

That weekend, the weather was not postcard wonderful, but we made the best of it as we settled in to enjoy our change of pace. I had booked us an excursion to see the dolphins, and boy, did we ever see them! We ended that day by having dinner at the famous Guy Fieri's Chophouse. (I was clearly not plant-based that day and not anywhere close to being *stegan*. Tracey was in charge and loving it.)

Our amazing dinner now over, we went back to the hotel and were talking about the great day we had, when we realized how thin the walls were. Next door to us was a couple in the midst of a huge argument. The woman was upset that the man had drunk so much at dinner. Ed and I listened in silence as their words began flowing back and forth like angry ocean waves in a tumultuous storm.

I instantly felt the hairs on the back of my neck stand up. The scene in the next room had me recalling a time when I was married to my ex, ending a day just like this while on vacation—in a miserable argument that had me in pieces. Ed and I looked at each other as images of our own past marriages surfaced. He, too, had left an unhappy situation. We held each other in silence and thought how fortunate we were that we were no longer in that place. If the universe put that couple next to us as a reminder of our journey, we got the message.

For hours, the scene next door escalated. Finally, we could hear the woman crying hysterically and sobbing until she succumbed to sleep. But the next morning, it started all over again. I couldn't pretend to be shocked. Once upon a time, I was that woman. As I shook off the dark memories, I wondered how many people were out there stuck in loveless, toxic relationships.

In that moment, I remember feeling so grateful for having made the decision to leap. For me, the fear of remaining in my situation was more powerful than the fear of being alone. Facing death was the only catalyst that helped me make that move. Hearing that interaction reminded me of how precious every moment is and how we all deserve to be treated with decency and respect, even if the union between two people is broken. We are all worth it. And this is why we are here on Earth: to be happy and feel love.

ACKNOWLEDGMENTS

could write an entire book about all of the amazing people who have been a part of this journey with me. *Gratitude* is not a strong enough word to describe how I feel. With that said, I do want to specifically thank a few people who have been the wind beneath my wings: my mom, Bobbi Lehrer, who has guided me since the day I was born to push past what's possible. My dad, Howard Lehrer (may he rest in peace) who taught me to never give up. My daughter, Sabrina, who inspires me every single day. My amazing husband, Ed Domanico, who showed me what true love and a supportive partner looks like. My sister, Debra Genender, who has been my biggest cheerleader. My stepmother, Ellen Gottlieb, who has shaped my life in so many ways. My crazy sorority sisters Watson and Tinkerbell, who answered my equally crazy texts at all hours when ideas popped into my head. Kim Mackey, who has been a continuous source of support from the beginning and an incredible friend. Donna P., whose friendship and support I treasure. Chris Baron, who sent me a text one New Year's Day that said: *Write your story.* I'm so happy I listened. Michele Phillips and Lisa Brooks-Greaux, who inspired me to pursue my passion and then showed me how. Leigh Anne Lanier, who was one of the best leaders I have ever had the honor of working with and a great support when I needed to make hard decisions. And Alex, who has become a mentor and a friend.

ABOUT THE AUTHOR

Known by many for asking the question that would become the title of her book, Stacey Aaron Domanico is a certified life and empowerment coach. Her love for mentoring and public speaking began decades ago within the context of her successful career of more than twenty-five years in corporate America with a Fortune-50-company. A surthriver (thriving survivor) of advanced breast cancer and other life-altering challenges, Stacey offers inspirational and actionable tools and tips in *Where Do You Spend Your Heartbeats?* with which to lovingly nudge her readers to design the lives of their dreams, instead of waiting for a catastrophic event to kickstart their journeys. A proud New Yorker by birth who still can't resist a great thin-crust pizza, today she is living her dream life in New Jersey with her husband, Ed, their four children, and fur baby, Bella.

Stacey Aaron Domanico
Coaching LLC
1 (862) 258-5614
info@coachingwithstacey.com
www.coachingwithstacey.com

photo by: Erin Usawicz Photography